AF323776

A CIP catalogue of this book is available from the National Library of Australia.

Messenger, Lisa
Break-ups & Breakthroughs
ISBN: 978-0-9943109-6-5

First published in 2016 by The Messenger Group Pty Ltd
PO Box H241
Australia Square NSW 1215

Editors: Kate Creevey, Mel Carswell and Jen Taylor
Proof readers and editorial support: Rebecca Hanley, Melanie Dimmitt and Tara Francis
Production Manager: Jade Dunwoody
Book design: Edith Swan
Photography of Lisa: Scott Ehler
Lisa H&MU: Giorgia Skye
Lisa styling: Alex de Jong
Lisa clothing: Spell & The Gypsy Collective
Lisa jewellery: MANIAMANIA
PR Manager: Jessica Stones, jessica@collectivehub.com
Distribution enquiries: Claire Belbeck, claire@collectivehub.com

This is proudly a Collective Hub product
collectivehub.com

Please enjoy every word in this book, but do not misinterpret it for professional, expert advice on matters as important as your health and wellbeing. If you feel you need extra support at any time, please speak to a professional. – Lisa x

BREAK-UPS & breakthroughs

turn an ending into a beginning

To my team at Collective Hub

because you are frickin' awesome

and no matter what comes your way, or what idea
I throw at you (like hey, let's write a book about
my hideous break-up), you jump at it.

You are like family and I'm grateful for you every single day.
Let's keep changing the world together.

introduction

I thought my next book might be entitled *Marriage & Motherhood,* but life had other plans. After all, I was deeply in love with the man of my absolute dreams and the ring on my finger only confirmed it. We'd mapped out our goals for life, discussed our stance on the world and had endless midnight musings about how our days would unfold until we were grey and wrinkly. We'd talked politics, religion, philosophy and sex; and hashed out plans for the immediate future down to the microscopic details of how we'd juggle 'everyday life' with our respective, exploding and somewhat public businesses. This was no summer fling or rebound relationship. This was a deep spiritual, emotional and physical connection; a tale of soul mates finally found. This was meant to be IT and he was meant to be THE ONE, whereby in good and bad times we would honestly and authentically be by each other's side – we'd do our best to forgive, understand, overcome and propel each other forward to be the best version of ourselves that we could possibly be. We would have each other's backs, even on those tough, crappy days.

Clearly the universe didn't get the memo. Didn't it know how long I had waited for something of this value, how much work I had done on myself to this point, how much of myself I had invested into it, how perfect it seemed or how euphoric it felt? No, life had a *drastically* alternate plan and whether I was in agreement or not, I would be thrust onto a horrendous ride that would nearly break me. I would succumb to *the one* thing that none of us is immune to, the one thing we can't escape no matter how strong, together, funny or fabulous we are – heartbreak.

A study of women estimates that we will endure two intense break-ups and there's varying research to suggest we'll have multiple meaningful relationships before we'll find *the one*. I'd come out the other side of long-term relationships in the past in a matter of days, but not this time. Perhaps because it was so unexpected and so sudden, maybe because of the promise that had come with it, or the fact that the two things I held most sacred – respect and loyalty – were stripped away in an instant. Possibly because of its public nature – tens of thousands of people knew about it from our personal and business profiles. More likely, it was a combination of all of these. Heartbreak is a terrible state of confliction and it is difficult to be distracted from the pain. At times, it feels easier and even comforting to dwell in it. You miss the little things – that smiley face when you first wake up, the text messages or one-sentence emails throughout the day saying, "I love you" in a zillion different ways, or those silly, idiosyncratic things that made you an 'us'. I knew people were suffering far worse than I was in all manner of life situations and were overcoming challenges to a magnitude that I would never face, but in every moment, everything is always relative. The process of a break-up is not linear – you go through different phases of dark emotional pain including grief, fear, loneliness, rage, jealousy, vengefulness, scorn and humiliation. At the start, it's all you can do to breathe, get out of bed, take one bite of anything or manage a foot outside the front door.

So here I was, six months after the marriage proposal of the century, which rolled out over 24 hours, across three locations and cost an awful lot to achieve – the sort that had every girl drooling and every man wondering how he'd ever match it. I was sitting in my living room with tears rolling down my cheeks as I replaced the words in my notebook from "Marriage & Motherhood" to "Break-ups & Breakthroughs". How did I get here?

Thoughts still darted through my mind like arrows – fear, uncertainty, but mostly a lot of "what the hell just happened?" Emotions pulsated through my body. Tears fell at the memories we had made and the stories we had told. It was still so very raw – I was far from healed and I was certainly not yet restored; the break-up songs of Taylor Swift and Whitney Houston still on repeat in the background. *Why* would I write such a seemingly personal book on the back of such a difficult time? Why would I do that to myself? It was simple, and I was resolute in my decision, as hard as it was. I made a conscious choice a few years ago to live my fullest life, completely true to my purpose, to be an inspiration and example to others in both the good and the excruciatingly difficult times. I would live my life daringly and ferociously, out loud, demonstrating to others that anything was – and is – possible.

Everything I loved, breathed, passed through or experienced would be fodder to share, impart, strengthen, encourage and empower. I would not be afraid to live with vulnerability and authenticity, whatever life threw at me. So when this curveball arrived in all its heart-breaking glory, there was no choice as to whether or not I would talk about it openly. I had already decided that in everything I did, I would live it, learn from it and share about it. I must say that in the year after our break-up, not a bad word was uttered publicly about him and that was a conscious choice, if a little difficult at times. Even now, it's not easy to pen this story, but it is important, otherwise you'd never understand the value and journey behind the 50 steps that are to come in this book.

     BREAK-UPS & BREAKTHROUGHS

I am not immune from hurt and pain, and there most certainly was a time
I thought something like this would kill me. It sure made me buckle at the
knees, cry gallons of tears, be drenched in fear and forget to eat, but I wasn't
fully crushed by its weight or overcome by its power – and neither will you be.
Break-ups *are* hard (ugh) but no matter where you are in your journey right
now, I want to whisper gently into your soul in this moment that you will get
up and you will move forward again – even if that means one small step each day
towards freedom and health – because sunshine is truly on its way to wash away
this sh*tty day.

Perhaps your break-up has only just happened and you are thinking this is all
too much to digest in this moment – you can't even get to the kitchen right now
without falling in a mess on the way – or perhaps you're still daydreaming of
clawing your ex's eyes out (the little sh*t). Maybe right now you're thinking,
"Please Lisa Messenger, go away with your you-can-do-it, life-will-be-okay, get-
up-when-you-fall message." If that's you, I totally get it, but before you slam
this book shut, let me tell you a bit of my story...

I didn't expect the love of my life to walk out six days after we had just moved
into our dream apartment together. That he would do that five weeks after my
book *Life & Love* (that I had dedicated to him…) went on sale globally, and for
which I was just starting a heavy publicity schedule. Take a moment to imagine
that – I'm giving press interviews daily about LOVE in the midst of the most
horrific break-up of my life. The book became the #1 seller on one of Australia's
biggest online retailers just three weeks into the sale period, which should have
been a career-fulfilling dream, only to be completely marred by the uncertainty
of my relationship status. I didn't expect him to walk in the door from work one
afternoon, suggest I take the dog for a walk and then simply vanish from our lives
without explanation or much communication for weeks.

I didn't know where to put myself.
I didn't know how to be.
I didn't know what to do.

The next morning, I had to have a fairly major procedure on my leg and after a completely sleepless night (you know the ones where you wake bolt upright in bed gasping for air), I laid down on the operating table. When the doctor offered me gas for pain relief, for the first time in my life I grabbed that mouthpiece and sucked on it for dear life as tears rolled down my cheeks. I sobbed and sobbed and sobbed. I didn't care what they were doing to my leg – the tears were not for that and no physical pain could ever have compared to what I was experiencing deep inside. I was utterly broken.

Because of work there was little opportunity to stop – I run a magazine distributed into 37 countries and a content-generating company operating across multiple platforms which was in an aggressive growth phase at the time. So I kept going – I had to. I kept turning up. I kept shaking hands. I kept speaking to crowds. I kept giving motivational speeches (they were authentic though, I believed in what I was saying and never once tried to misconstrue anything). That was such a hard part to contend with – being so open about my life and journey so publicly, right in the middle of 'it' at that moment. It wasn't a divorce a decade earlier or the stories of how alcohol almost ruined my life in my mid-twenties – this was my life *right now* and I wasn't in control of a rather large chunk of it. Yet, I still had to get up and attempt to inspire others each day. I kept running my business. I kept leading my staff. The day after that operation, I attended an event in Melbourne then flew to Fiji for a family gathering for my mum's seventieth and after that, I jumped on a flight to New York City to broker what would be the biggest deal of my life to date. Things kept coming at me and for eight weeks, I simultaneously lived the best life imaginable (that NYC deal was a lifetime in the making and one I am so very proud of) and the most painful one imaginable. In hindsight, I have absolutely no idea how I functioned so 'normally' for months.

Due to the public nature of our relationship (and particularly my growing presence on social media, numbering in the tens of thousands) it was impossible to escape people's well-wishes every single day. Being in the magazine business, we are often showered with gifts, from the latest health-fad-inspired breakfast bars to premium moisturisers launching next month, graffiti-covered surfboards and Fairtrade shoes, and my office is the first stop for everything that comes through our doors. Beyond the normal bounds of the magazine, gifts were flooding in from friends and followers all over the world (thousands who we had never met) to help celebrate our engagement – and it should have been wonderful (in some ways it still was – I was completely floored at people's kindness and generosity).

I hadn't told people we'd broken up, because I didn't know for sure if we had. So in came the gifts each day, sent with wonderful and generous intention, only to arrive as a daily reminder of the hell I was living. I was even sent a pair of lace knickers with my proposed married name embroidered across the bum (sorry to the maker if you are reading this – the thought was lovely). There were the dainty wedding shoes in my correct size, a hand-cut 'circle of life' butterfly artwork, the his-and-her clothes, honeymoon offers, personalised cushion covers and the engraved jewellery (we have plenty of monogrammed gear if anyone matches the initials…).

Then there was the movie I went to see with a friend. She had been trying to get pregnant for ages and had received yet another disappointing result from her IVF and, in the midst of my break-up, I had suffered a miscarriage so the topic of children was very raw and real for us both. My friend suggested we watch a movie about the Spanish Camino de Santiago trail that she hoped to trek. Turns out, she had the time and date wrong so instead we watched *TED 2*, a movie about a teddy bear who was trying to get his wife pregnant… it could not have been more inappropriate – we both ended up crying desperately, but then we laughed hysterically at the craziness of our lives.

After managing to completely avoid knowing anything (and I mean nothing) about my ex during that difficult time, I came home one night to see my cleaner mopping the floor. She proceeded to give me a blow-by-blow description of exactly where he was living, what he was doing and who he was doing it with. Somehow I was saved (sort of) by her thick accent, my loud protestations, a sudden case of Tourette's and an attempt at profound deafness for the entire tirade. Seriously, we have thousands of Facebook friends between us and I'd managed to stay blissfully ignorant of what he'd been up to, only to be bailed up in my own home by my cleaner who seemed to have a bad case of 'can't shut the fu*k up...'

There was the fact that I, a health nut and exercise lover, was for the first time in my life basically surviving on sleeping pills and cigarettes. (Yes, I KNOW!)

There was the day two friends came over and literally had to force-feed me while I wiped snot from my face. Correction: I am pretty sure they wiped it away. They also tried to give me a glass of water, which I accidentally knocked out of their hands and smashed on the floor. I didn't care. I don't even know who cleaned that up, to be honest. I could not move.

There was the fact that I lost more than a sixth of my body weight during those first few months.

Then there was the wedding I sat through on a table of 10 with one spare seat – my plus one. His entrée arrived. "Oh no, there is no one sitting there," I say. Then the main course arrives. "No, still no one sitting there," I tell the same waiter. By dessert, it was comical. "Yep, pretty sure eight weeks after he walked out with no explanation, that this isn't the time he's going to choose to make a miraculous re-appearance!" The poor waiter ran away as fast as he could and probably downed a glass of champagne in the kitchen on my behalf. It was a really beautiful wedding (congratulations my dear friends), but I watched them have their first dance, burst into tears and gently removed myself from the situation.

And then, there was the day when just as I had begun to forget all about this hot mess, hundreds of shocked friends and acquaintances contacted me when he appeared in a magazine 'bachelor of the year' competition. I am pretty sure my phone almost broke from the traffic! I am sure he wouldn't have drawn the parallel, but it was the same week that our baby would have been born.

So that was it. A life thrust into (very) unexpected turmoil. It happened. And it *hurt.* And in the past, I would beat myself up saying, "I could have done this or that better" and I was right. But this time, I could honestly say – hand on heart – I was the best version of myself that I could possibly have been and perhaps that is why it was more shocking and painful. But, this book isn't a bitch fest or a "let's get angry and even" foray. I wish him the best in his life and know that better days are ahead. He no doubt has his own version. This is simply my story and it's not something I choose to embroil myself in energetically or something that will have a hold over me for the rest of my days. I really want to stress that it's *not about the story* – to be honest, I'm so over the story; it now bores me to tears! I'm not interested in re-living it, rehashing it or giving it any more energy. This is about a conscious choice I made in all that pain and grief to celebrate the incredible life I had created – and worked so hard for in the days that led to that moment – and to find a way to continue to live with gratitude, dignity and grace through it all.

I somehow found a way through all the sh*t, disbelief and disappointment to grieve and cry but also to dig deep and harness the tools to keep going – and I did it because I knew unequivocally, in the depths of my soul, what my 'why' was for life; that I was to live my life out loud and be an entrepreneur for entrepreneurs, to inspire and encourage others to live their best life. So even when I was a mess on the floor, crying in the bottom of the shower or struggling to get out of bed when I had 9am meetings at the office, even in my depths, I knew I was stronger than I had been in any other moment in my life. I clung with my fists gripped so firmly to the truth that adversity and hard times can be the biggest catalyst for change, for lifting, for truly living our lives with integrity and authenticity if we let them. And for that response in the midst of such deep heartache, I have to say, it's the proudest I've ever been of myself.

Between the tissues and unattractive crying sessions (you know the ones), I saw an opportunity to grow. It forced me to look at my failings, character defects and insecurities all over again, chipping away at each a little more to be the best version of myself. As painful as it was, that was an up-shot that propelled me forward.

I thought I had done a lot of 'work' on myself up until that point to remove fear from my life. For years prior, I had confidently said I had none, but suddenly I found myself almost crippled by fear – not in a business sense; that part was easy-ish (or so it suddenly seemed against the backdrop of what I was enduring), but fear of losing something I had cherished so deeply, fear about undoing all the life plans we had created, fear of how to handle something that had become quite public, fear around how it would unfold when our businesses were in such a similar space, but above all, fear of being at the centre of something that was beyond my control. And that kept coming at me from all kinds of unexpected directions. (While fears of being alone are real and I had felt them much earlier in my life, I was not worried about that now. I always knew I was going to be okay because I had created a life that I loved; because there was life before him and there would most certainly and unquestionably be life after him).

However fear unfolds in our lives, it is real and must be felt, but then it must also be dealt with swiftly. So, on a sweet Saturday morning I looked up at the universe and whispered the words, "thank you". Thanks to all that personal development, I really did know that fear was irrational, unhealthy and unhelpful, and that I had a choice – I needed to take a hold of the situation and systematically find a way out or I would be the one to lose in the long term. I thanked the universe for the opportunity to grow and learn on an entirely new level. Love is volatile and this was not just about me but another human who seemed to have lost his way and was going through real fears of his own.

In the end, it was also fear that kept me from sharing the news publicly for almost four months – I was fearful about not being authentic with everyone around me, when I am such an advocate of that and had chosen to live my life openly, but I wasn't trying to hide anything – for much of that time I had no idea what was going on, if it would be fixed or if it would end forever. For the first two months, only seven people knew. That was tough, but at the same time sensible and the best thing I could have done. I needed to know that it was truly over. Then I needed to gather myself and be ready to deal with what that meant for me personally and publicly – after all, my book had only been on sale for a few months and included details of our relationship and proposal. Do I regret that book? Not at all! The day it went to print was the day I noticed he started to change and in my mind, lose his way.

Until that point, it truly was the most magical fairytale and larger-than-life love between us. I had never felt so adored and I don't regret including him in the book, for at the time it was incredible and so was he. I've since rewritten parts of *Life & Love* and generalised some of the content, but I certainly wouldn't erase the experience from my overall love experience because it was real, and from all the feedback I received on the first 10,000 copies, hardly anyone mentioned the components about our love story – the feedback was always directed at the areas that helped and empowered others. As it is about living a full life in all areas and riding the bumps to enjoy the sunshine, I know now more than ever that I have earned my place to write it.

Whether a break-up hits you like a bolt of lightning or you were the one to inflict the storm, a lifetime of history led you to that point, and as soon as I reconciled that thought I was ready to share the news. It had held me down, kept my thinking small and controlled me in ways I never thought possible. So, I shared one public message and that was it.

I will probably never know the reason he walked out that day and I'm okay with that. (In my mind, he was on the run and, having had this pattern of behaviour in my own past, I had some compassion and understanding of it in a way, just coupled with an immense sadness that he was unable to pull himself out of it – we are all human beings who love and bleed and hurt.) After sharing the news, I was inundated with thousands of messages. It was an unexpected and incredibly humbling barrage – and it showed me, yet again, that I had made it my mission to help others and to empower them in whatever I was doing. There, the seeds of *Break-ups & Breakthroughs* were firmly planted in my soul.

This book is an insight into my own healing, the tools learned over a lifetime and gathered from friends new and old that helped restore and sustain me during

     BREAK-UPS & BREAKTHROUGHS

this time. It is a combination of many years of personal development, drawing from many books I've read, courses I've done and experiences I've had, which have given me the tools to break through and move forward, even when it felt impossible to do so. It is unlike all of my other books, which were written more in retrospect. This, instead, was written in the moment, with the backdrop being exactly what I was experiencing at the time. As a result, the writing is lighter in places, crafted to be more helpful and comforting to a fragile soul than to bog you down with meatier philosophies. I am perpetually fascinated by the human psyche when it comes to relationships, so perhaps there will be another book that goes a little deeper, down the track. But for now… I hope the steps to healing in the following pages are exactly what you need. You won't find much more about my personal life in the rest of these pages – I have said all I need to. Nor will you find anger or hurt. Instead, I hope these resources, positive affirmations, quotes, tips, meditations, exercises, advice from friends and gorgeous, uplifting pictures will feed your soul and help you return to a place of peace and purpose.

Life throws us curve balls.
I had a fiancé and I was in love.
Then I didn't and I wasn't.

But then we start all over again. We form new habits (which I find fascinating!) and we fill the space, each day building a new, enhanced hybrid of ourselves. Then one day you realise that you've just seen or heard something about your ex and you're like, 'meh', and just like that you're over the addictive quality that seems to attach itself to sadness and heartbreak. You feel the warmth of sunshine on your back and a lightness in your soul, for your healing has really begun.

Life throws us sh*t and that is never going to stop, no matter how intelligent, brave or optimistic we are, but it's how we handle it that really defines us. At every turn is a choice and we can consciously choose grace and dignity every single day. Over the next few pages you will find 50 steps to help you on your journey, divided into the four key phases which I personally encountered in my own break-up. They are: survival, acceptance, nourishment and renewal. I hope the words in this book comfort you when you cry, embrace you like a warm blanket, inspire you to return to greatness and overall, help you find your inner glow once again.

Perhaps the best advice I personally received was this: surround yourself with strong, amazing, powerful men and fabulous, soft, vulnerable women as you go. Be kind to yourself constantly. Practise self-love. Be careful who you give power and energy to and above all else, take back control of the narrative of your life. Because only one person can live it: YOU. And don't give up on love – truly believe in it as you develop yourself as a strong, independent person. For all of the rest, you'll have to read on…

Lisa xx

CONTENTS

acceptance

nourishment

survival

01.

GET OUT OF BED

Sounds easy enough. But when you're broken apart on the inside and just want the peace that only oblivion or amnesia can bring, the very thought of that upward, I-need-to-face-the-world-today feeling is enough to send you slumping back under the covers in search of your tissues and misery. After all, shutting out the world with all its pain and harsh reality (how could it be so cruel?) is so much easier.

So here's the tip: force yourself to get out of bed twice a day, even if it's just for half an hour, and even if your body and soul feel unbearably heavy. To do what, you ask? It doesn't really matter, the strength is in the 'doing', as if you're shouting to the world that this won't beat your broken self, not today, not ever. And that small step, in all its seeming nothingness, is the powerful beginning of a journey towards healing and empowerment that really does exist, even if you can't see it right now.

Go for a walk, pat the dog, put on some music, attempt to make yourself a pot of tea (even if it smashes on the floor by accident, which happened to me on day three – and stayed broken on the floor for another two days). Stand in the fresh air, cry in the backyard, sit in the rain, look up, lay on the grass or go get yourself a coffee under the cover of big sunglasses, which you probably won't drink, but at least you are out – at least you are moving.

It's completely fine to slump back into bed when you need to, but more often than not, the interruption will be enough to help you push through the grief and initial torpor, and make you feel better, stronger and more able to face the day and your new reality (even for a moment). If you can't get yourself moving today, don't be too hard on yourself, but encourage yourself to try and attempt it tomorrow.

Be mindful that we often feel most vulnerable and alone under the cloak of darkness – late at night or very early in the morning. This is a good time to force yourself out of bed to break the stronghold, even if all you do is wander around the house and back to the covers or couch again. Put one foot in front of the other, and acknowledge yourself as you do. Feel proud of yourself for taking that one small step and rising to the challenge.

          BREAK-UPS & BREAKTHROUGHS

it's completely FINE to slump back into BED.
*(when you need to)

02.

NOURISH YOURSELF

Your stomach is in a tangled mess, right? Often in those first few days after the person who was once the centre of your world has been, literally, ripped out of your world, your stomach is in such knotted chaos that putting food into it seems impossible. And while the 'break-up diet' can seem like one of the few upsides of the whole heart-achy mess, there is definitely such a thing as too much. Sometimes when you think you're fabulously slim, others see you as unhealthily skinny, and at this time, their eyes might be more objective than yours.

I lost a sixth of my body weight with this last break-up and let me tell you, it wasn't fun or healthy – I had to force-feed myself some days. The few friends who knew what had happened would pop over with home-cooked meals, or even takeaway they had grabbed especially for me on their way home from work. One of my staff members noticed and started dropping food on my desk. Sounds hopeless, doesn't it? But in that moment I was a little lost and food was the very last thing on my mind. It is, however, important to listen to your friends if they kindly mention you look a little gaunt.

Treating your body with kindness and respect is one of the best ways to heal yourself, and it is also physically essential. Physical strength and mental and emotional stability are three things that will help see you through the tough times.

Any major life change or upheaval creates a massive shift in both your physical and energetic bodies, and a release of toxins is a by-product, especially where there is powerful emotional release. So, it is vital that you put things into your precious body that will allow this cleansing to occur gently but thoroughly, and that will keep you healthy.

To help this process, make sure you drink loads... of water, that is. Water is a non-negotiable, and if you can't stomach anything else or just don't feel like cooking, soups and smoothies – things that are warming and/or cleansing and easy to swallow – will nurture your body as you adjust to your new life.

Psychologists have suggested the apathy towards food that often accompanies a break-up typically lasts between 1 and 10 days. That means you *will* eventually feel like eating properly again.

At this stage of the break-up, your new partners, Mr Tim Tam or Miss Sauvignon Blanc, might be keeping you cosy on the couch – but before you let that fling turn into a fully fledged every-night-of-the-week partnership, remember after that initial escapist buzz, these flaky characters won't be there in the morning to wipe up your tears.

We all feel the urge to try and fill that empty crevasse in our hearts with comfort foods, but once you start to feel some semblance of normal again, the best thing you can do to aid your recovery is nurture yourself with foods that will up your strength and boost your mood. Keep drinking water; avoid sugar (if that aligns with your values) because sugar is one of the greatest depressants.

shopping list

BANANAS: These contain tryptophan, which can be converted into serotonin – one of the brain's feel-good chemicals – plus potassium, which is key to giving your body those boosts of energy.

SALMON: It contains omega-3s, which do wonders for your physical heart, plus selenium, low levels of which have links to depressive symptoms.

KEFIR: This fermented food is packed with probiotics, which soothe your gut (aka the second brain), and in turn reduce those up-and-down moods.

DARK CHOCOLATE: I'm not suggesting you banish chocolate from your pantry at peak break-up (that's just crazy talk), just stick to the dark stuff – it's lower in sugar and higher in cocoa, which has been shown to have beneficial effects on cardiovascular health. It actually helps prevent a (physical) broken heart.

03.

SLEEP TIGHT

Have you had those days in the aftermath, where you wake up so tired you could cry? Yep, often the more we need shut-eye in order to stay emotionally resilient, the more we find ourselves lying awake replaying that final conversation/text/ email on repeat in our heads.

Scientists have actually discovered there are physiological reasons for this irony: long-term couples start to regulate each other's biological rhythms, so when your ex is no longer on the other side of the bed, your body goes into confused mode. A break-up can have significant impacts on your heart rate, body temperature – and sleep.

I normally sleep 8 to 10 hours every night (I know… all my friends with insomnia or those with kids want to kill me when I mention that small detail) – so for me personally, heartbreak wrought havoc on my body's rhythm and balance. In the weeks following, I was waking bolt upright in the middle of the night with panic attacks (for the first time in years) and then could not sleep past dawn in the morning. It was not only debilitating, but as those who struggle with sleep know, you end up stressed because you know you need sleep to help keep your spirits high and to function the following day (big presentations, important meetings, simply managing business bumps), but you can't still your mind enough to get it. As a result, I was deliriously beside myself. It was horrible.

Break-up or no break-up, you simply cannot function effectively on any level without proper sleep, and it is said that during times of emotional trauma or deep grief, you should try and get at least two hours more sleep a night than you would normally. If you can force yourself to get into bed earlier, do. Take a good book if you need to – no devices or electronics, as the light they emit actually interferes with your ability to switch off and sleep.

For night owls this can be tricky, but one of the benefits of going to bed early is that late nights are usually the times when everything seems so much worse, so much harder, lonelier and more frightening.

Please don't underestimate the importance of prioritising healthy, restful sleep patterns (and no, this doesn't include scrolling through your camera roll in the wee hours looking at old pics of you two in the hope it will help you 'drift off'). What you really need to do is still those crazy thoughts and centre your yo-yo-ing mind. One of the best ways to do this is by incorporating meditation into your daily routine.

As renowned mediation teacher Tom Cronin says, meditation is a powerful way to restore sleep patterns. "Meditation isn't something we do when we have a calm mind – it leads to a calm mind," he says. "Our body is a print-out of our mind. Each day our minds are analysing, processing and digesting copious amounts of information. The level of data that our minds have to absorb is increasing at an exponential rate. This is the prime reason why insomnia is at an all-time high.

"Meditation is the most important step in the process of you being able to effortlessly fall asleep each night. Meditation is the tool that will give you control over that monkey mind, so when your head hits the pillow, your mind will surrender into the delicious stillness of sleep... Meditation is a simple exercise for your mind, just like going to the gym or a jog is for your body."

RESERVED

1. Sit comfortably upright in a chair

2. Close your eyes and take three deep breaths

3. Allow your breath to flow naturally, not forced, just your effortless breath

4. Draw your attention to the air as it moves through your nostrils and it slightly cools the skin around the rim of the nostrils

5. Keep your attention there for 5 to 10 minutes. Your mind will wander and drift away but keep bringing it back to this single point

6. After your time is up, just sit for a few moments, then slowly open your eyes

"Once you learn to meditate, it is recommended that you meditate twice a day, once in the morning before breakfast, and once in the afternoon or early evening before dinner," says Tom. "Ideally, meditate for 15 to 20 minutes each time."

The nutrients you consume can also play a huge role in how well you fall, and stay, asleep. In particular, magnesium – found in nuts, leafy vegetables, dark chocolate and bananas – is crucial for healthy sleep.

Another exercise to help you switch off quickly is the 4-7-8 breathing method. Simply breathe in for four counts, hold for seven counts, and then exhale for eight counts. According to experts, it has the power to send you to sleep in just 60 seconds!

You might find initially that you wake up at odd hours, like four in the morning. However, if you keep a notebook by the bed and just write down whatever thoughts or feelings are coming into your mind at that time, you should be able to sink back into sleep, and will wake feeling lighter, more energised and more able to deal with the day and your new reality.

     BREAK-UPS & BREAKTHROUGHS

my energy, is precious: i won't use it on matters of the past, only on things that will create a better me.

- LISA MESSENGER

04.

GET YOUR
PEEPS IN PLACE

As this horrendous process unfolds, it's important that you don't feel alone or unable to cope with what comes your way. As mentioned, it's also important to eat (beans on toast three nights in a row gets rather old). And eventually, you'll need someone to make you laugh about it all. Not too much, but just enough. What am I getting at here? The best thing you can do after a break-up is get your gang in order. Your posse. Your peeps. Your cheer squad. The crew that will prop you up when you need it, who will wipe the tears from your face when you've hit rock bottom, who will replenish the dishwashing detergent, who will buy the takeout, who will throw some tough love your way when you're ready, and who will tell you that you're smokin' hot when you start to question your worth. Here's a quick guide to the essential characters every break-up-ee needs; those people who will make your journey more bearable, and in retrospect, rather endearing.

THE CAREGIVERS

They walk your dog, mow your lawn, pick up your dirty clothes from the floor and take them to the dry cleaner. They pre-order the tissues, offer to be your plus-one at events, and swing via the office late just to hang, because they know you have a late meeting. Let these peeps do their thing; don't push back. When you're pretty angry at the world, they remind you of the kindness in humanity.

THE FEEDERS

They peel, chop, boil, stew or buy (unpacking takeout is just as important). You sit on the floor together and sip on green juice or push Rogan Josh around a plate while lamenting about the day's struggles.

THE TOUGH LOVERS

They tell you how it is without much of a filter. "Ohhhh, you were better off without them anyway," is the first thing they say. "Move on" is the next. Oh. Right. You're kind of left hanging on the phone, trying to digest it all. Don't call these people when you really need a crutch but do go to them when you secretly know the truth but need a voice of reason to confirm it or push you over the edge of acceptance.

THE MOVERS

They keep you going. They are the ones who knock on the door at 6am for a walk. They are taking a group rock climbing this weekend and propose you come. They suggest a swim even though it's winter. They say they'll come to you and they do. You walk, run, swim, climb and you don't even need to speak – they even let you cry and don't push you to talk about it. My tip when they call: say 'yes' (and later, buy them a gift for their kindness).

THE DIFFUSERS

The people who won't even entertain the drama or give it any energy. You mention something and they half walk off with a "pffft", followed by the line, "gosh, I wouldn't even worry about it, you're so much better off now." When you hear bad news and you know you want someone to brush if off, so you can, go to a Diffuser.

THE ROCKS

Rock-solid, nothing will shake them. You can go to them with anything and they will be calm, cool and 100 per cent collected. They do not peak or trough, but flat-line right in the middle of your life. Whatever you say to them, they will reply with exactly what you need, statements like, "you are better than this", "this won't beat you", "you've got this", "they are a little sh*t and you are better off without them" and "I have seen you beat more than this, this is nothing but a bump along a very long and awesome road". Feeling weak, fragile or questioning your own self-worth? Call a Rock.

THE BULLDOGS

Though these are friends, watch out for these people. They play a vital role in your life generally but in a time of crisis they can quickly become a foe. That's because they are the friends who are loaded with negative energy and love the drama of it all. It makes you instantly sick to the stomach when they call, not because you don't love them, but because they are the people who can't wait to call you when your ex posts a picture of themselves in bed late at night (ie someone else has taken that). They want the dirty details and they love a good gossip with you and everyone else. They are SO unhelpful. Avoid their calls and back away from the friendship for a time and when you are brave enough, have a frank chat with them about it, asking them to tone it down.

THE COTTON-WOOL BRIGADE

No matter what happens, these are the friends who will be there to listen and to soften any blow as it comes your way. They'll do anything they can to help shield you from the world until you are ready for it. They will tell you about your ex, but only when they think you need to know and do so gently and softly. When you break up with your ex, it is really hard to accept that you once knew everything about them before anyone else did. You were their first responder and now you are well and truly their last – and that is hard. Lean in to your cotton-wool brigade (especially after you see a missed call from a Bulldog and know there must be news in the wind). They have your back and will help you digest the information, good and bad.

THE HOT PLATONIC CONTINGENT

These are your gorgeous friends (inside and out) who will drag you out of the house to do stuff while constantly telling you that you are amazing. You know you will never, ever, ever 'go there' with them, but it's pretty darn nice being around attractive people when you're in pain, so they can make you laugh (because they will definitely do that), but to also have them say you are truly wonderful. When you're feeling down, or feel like love will elude you forever, call a Hot Platonic-er.

REPEAT AFTER ME:
i am brave. i am fearless.
i am strong. i am powerful.
- LISA MESSENGER

05.
BE KIND TO YOURSELF

be gentle with yourself. you're doing the best you can.

– ANONYMOUS

The day I announced our break-up, a wonderful friend sent me a message from across the globe. Part of it included these beautiful, practical words:

"Deep pain can slowly but surely etch itself into your dress and bearing. So, pamper yourself a little to offset this effect and to prevent you sending a negative message to yourself and others. Get regular massages, manicures, pedicures, hair appointments and facials (being touched gently really matters) and splurge a little on some nice things to wear that you've had your eye on. Don't go retail-therapy crazy, just remind yourself that you look good and you deserve to feel good too!"

What kind advice. It's yours for the taking…

06.

WALLOW IN IT

This step may come as a surprise to you because I am such a positive person, but no one can be rock solid in every moment of every day. I truly believe that most of the time, the best thing you can do for yourself is to be positive, to think positive thoughts and to generally manifest positivity in all that you do. But today, I give you full permission to toss the positive mantras and affirmations aside (for now). Cry yourself stupid and be held hostage in your grief – the inescapable, natural response to having someone you love wrenched from your life. Lie back and let the pain wash over you; cut yourself some slack and take an early mark on awesome… if only for the day.

In *The Wisdom of Insecurity*, Alan W Watts says, "I have discovered that pain and the effort to be separate from it are the same thing." In other words, the more we try and distract ourselves from pain, the longer it will take to escape it.

Now is not the time for keeping it cool. If you try to hide from this initial rush of raw emotion and play the "I'm fine" line, you're only delaying the healing

tears are better than OKAY, they are part of your RECOVERY.
think of them as your heart sweating out the poison of pain, anger, grief and despair.
- LISA MESSENGER

process. Ignoring your true feelings at this point is like closing the door on a house fire… you have no idea when that baby's going to blow. So feel the burn and get it out. NOW.

Take the time, a day or two off work (a month, even), and feel this for what it is – a really, really sh*tty, short period of your life that will start getting better once you've clambered your way through these first hours and days in a real, authentic way. Close off the world and bawl your eyes dry. Wrestle yourself ragged with shameless, indulgent, paralysing emotion. Because you know what? When you crawl out from under the covers and come out the other end, you've got work to do.

07.

HAVE A TECH DETOX

Oh to break up in the '80s, when a humble home phone attached to a wall presented the only portal of connection with your ex. Or better still, in Jane Austen's era, when a brush with your former beloved would only come with the great effort of wheeling out your horse and carriage and chancing on them at their estate. Not us! As our modern-day relationships end, we are hazardously surrounded by technology that's rife with emotional landmines presenting as hashtags, Facebook flashbacks and all manner of smartphone alerts. Then there's that excruciating moment when your ex selects 'single' on their Facebook profile and suddenly the entire world is privy to your heartache with one click and without your consent.

It has been suggested that almost half of us have slept with our phones, making it even more important to deal with your tech before every 'ding' makes you want to wail like Bridget Jones. Instead, go on a total tech detox. This cancels out any threat of 'seeing' your ex or being exposed to anything even remotely related to them (you'll be amazed at how clever and, subsequently, soul-destroying social media algorithms can be).

out of
sight
out of
mind

1. DELETE THEIR NUMBER FROM YOUR PHONE

One good thing about living in the digital age is that more often than not, we don't actually know anyone's actual phone number – they are just programmed into our devices. This also reduces the chance of the drunken dial or not-so-subtle, "So, how's it going?" text. But if you still share responsibilities (children, pets…) or really can't bring yourself to hit delete just yet, try changing their name in your contacts. Whenever I saw my ex's name flash up on my phone when we were together, my heart skipped a beat. After our break-up, he went through a stage of texting me a lot (that's a whole different section), so I really needed to cut the false excitement those texts brought. A great way to shift that energy is to change their name to something that will make you laugh or give you strength like, "Don't do it!" or "The Prick Is Calling!" There's always "Arsehole" for those early, angry days but be sure to eventually delete it altogether. Get. Rid. Of. It. Temptation gone. Energy cut.

2. TAKE A BREAK FROM ALL SOCIAL MEDIA, IF YOUR JOB ALLOWS IT

This gives you some space to re-group without the noise of hundreds or thousands of friends and the happenings of their lives. It also ensures that you won't stumble across news of your ex accidentally. For me personally, I had a social media community that I didn't want to abandon. So, I would jump on and post whatever was essential during that period, but I didn't look at anything else, AT ALL. That was a saving grace for me. Also, no matter how much you love your friends, you're probably not going to feel great about pictures or posts of their romantic getaway, baby's first steps or wedding anniversary dinner right now. And then you're going to feel bad for not feeling good about it. You don't need that.

3. WHEN YOU ARE READY TO RETURN TO SOCIAL MEDIA, IT'S TIME TO UNFRIEND AND UNFOLLOW

A simple click across your platforms can save you weeks, months or years of empty stalking and fruitless trips down memory lane. Once you've dealt with the mother ship, it's time to clear out the pawns. Unfriend (or at the very least, unfollow) close allies of your ex who are likely to share posts and pictures where they might make a cameo. Out of sight, out of mind. Or at least out of your feeds, for now. And now that you've got your social sphere to yourself, don't overshare. There's nothing enigmatic about a #shouldveputaringonit hashtag or passive-aggressive statements like, "The saddest thing about betrayal is that it never comes from your enemies." No matter how many positive comments and smiling emojis you might get in return, they're not worth your dignity. I opted for one simple post, then it was DONE. Energetically dealt with in that public space. Over. I didn't utter a single spoken word about it publicly from then, until this book.

4. CLEAN UP YOUR SOCIAL MEDIA ACCOUNTS

Finally, update your relationship status on platforms that include it and consider deleting albums of photos from your social media accounts with your ex in them. I didn't do this, I just left the past in the past, but it can be a cathartic exercise for some.

For those who love a bit of tech, there is a wealth of apps out there to help your cause, like Block Your Ex, Designated Dialer, Ex Lover Blocker and by the time of print, there will no doubt be more!

08.
REMOVE MEMORY TRIGGERS

Walking by the picture on the refrigerator every day of you two on holiday
in Spain that one time when you ate ice-cream and laughed until 2am about
your childhood is not going to make you happy now. Nor is opening up the
bathroom cupboard each morning to see their toiletries staring back at you. It's
hard to go to sleep at night and smell their scent on the bed sheets, to walk past
the watch on the dresser that they bought for you or even turn on the TV to see
their programmed 'profile'. When you are ready, start to systematically remove
memory triggers from your home and office – any space that is sacred to you.

Obviously, if you have small children they cannot be removed! But, there
are many things within your power that you'll do best without and you'll be
surprised at how helpful something so practical can be for your peace of mind.
Memories can be triggered by the obvious – their toothbrush   but also by the
smallest of things – their favourite chair or a playlist on your iPhone.

We have tens of thousands of thoughts every single day and your ex will already
be on your mind (consuming 90 per cent of it in those early days), so why not
give your mind a fighting chance by altering your environment? There are many
more, and there will be plenty unique to you, but here are three things to start
with to free your space and usher in the 'new':

1. DO A HOUSE CLEANSE

Enlist a trusted friend to help you go through each room and remove things
from your home that will trigger difficult memories of your ex. I cannot warn
you enough how hard this will be and that is where the friend comes in. You'll
need their moral support, someone to sit with you on the floor and talk about
"that baseball you bought in NYC at the Yankees game", and someone to laugh
with hysterically, which will turn into tears, when you find those awful shoes
they bought you for your first birthday together. Create a 'goodbye' box to

ritually throw in the trash, box it up to deal with later if you're not quite ready yet, sell items online (check out the website Never Liked It Anyway, which is devoted to this very situation) or donate anything suitable to charity. For something more substantial, move your furniture around, put new art on the walls, switch bedrooms or perform a cleansing ceremony with white sage. (My ex left everything in our home for four months afterwards, except a suitcase. Note to self: I should have done my cleanse sooner.)

2. CHANGE THE SHEETS

Intimacy carries with it great power and a strong energy. While changing the sheets on your bed sounds simple in theory, it can come with a lot of grief. Take your time and do it when you are ready or sleep in the spare room or on the couch for a while, if that is an option for you. (It was three weeks before I could venture back into 'our' room.)

3. CREATE A NEW ROUTINE

If you always went for a walk together before breakfast or slumped on the couch at exactly the same time every week for a favourite TV show (re-runs of *Friends,* anyone?), then continuing to do those things will only trigger thoughts of loss and loneliness. Strategically change your rituals: eat breakfast and then train, listen to a completely new genre of music, buy your green smoothie from a different cafe, get a new TV show and make a new meal (Saturday dinner instead of Saturday brunch) your new weekend highlight. Sounds too simple but trust me – your thought-life and ultimately, your heart, will thank you for the subtle changes.

your **space** should reflect who you are **today** not who you were **yesterday.**

– LISA MESSENGER

09.
EMBRACE THE EMOTIONAL
ROLLERCOASTER

A break-up is far from death and destruction, and I'll be the first to say that so many people endure much harder, more catastrophic, inhumane and gut-wrenching tragedies in their lives. BUT… in the midst of all that yuck, it's hard to be rational. And, even though no one has actually died on you, the end of a relationship is the death of something. Final. Over. Finished. Kaput. Gone.

Sorry! I can see you grabbing for the tissues or perhaps it's a dinner plate and you're about to throw it my way… but that bit of honest love is only to preface this key point: in the midst of a break-up, you'll most likely go through a few stages of grief (sometimes more than once), which are extremely similar to those Elisabeth Kübler-Ross famously penned in her groundbreaking book *On Death and Dying* in 1969. Accepting that these stages are real, normal and even healthy, makes it easier to actually digest them as they unfold. If you're up for a laugh, go watch Dr Hibbert tell Homer Simpson that he is going to die in 24 hours after eating a poisonous blowfish – "Now a little death anxiety is normal…" he begins. But on a more serious note, here are the stages and a few practical tips on each:

1. DENIAL: It's all about your heart at this point and you're not really interested in rational thought. You'll look for anything, even the tiniest thought that would suggest things will go back to 'normal'. This is when you should grab your best friends for support and stay away from alcohol-related philosophy and late-night texting.

2. ANGER: At them, at yourself, at life, at the universe, at anyone who disagrees with you, at the postman, at everyone. Just let it run its course, and try not to make any big or bad decisions in the process. Stay off social media and guard yourself against reuniting prematurely or casual sex (which is rarely a proud achievement or something that will make you happy in the long run).

3. BARGAINING: Even the smartest, most rational, 'together' people
will find a small corner of their brain where bargaining is deemed acceptable
at this point. Just think of your poor friends because this is when you try and
convince them that you are right or it is right. For those who believe in a higher
power, this is when the 'if they come back I will be a better person' prayers
also surface, which aren't all bad. Avoid reconnecting with your ex at this point
because you are vulnerable to accepting anything to reunite and that can be
dangerous on many levels.

4. DEPRESSION: Uh-huh. This is horrible and can manifest itself
into your life and mind in so many ways; lethargy, loss of appetite or over-
eating, insomnia (one of the many side effects I experienced personally), being
constantly on the edge of tears, feeling very fragile or ultimately, feeling that
all hope is gone for your relationship or worse, your life. Be incredibly kind to
yourself here and enlist the help of respectful people to gently keep you upright
and moving forwards. If you feel that it is all too much, don't hesitate to see a
counsellor or professional because you can never be too careful when it comes
to your mental health.

5. ACCEPTANCE: There is great beauty here; you begin to smile from
deep in your belly again and there is a tiny spring in your step, even if you won't
admit it to the world just yet. It's like the first day after a bad flu when it suddenly
dawns on you that you haven't sneezed all morning or broken out in one single
hot sweat; that you actually, hang on, you feel... okay. Know that this day in your
own cycle of grief is coming, and while there will still be extreme sadness, you'll
be okay with that, and with it all.

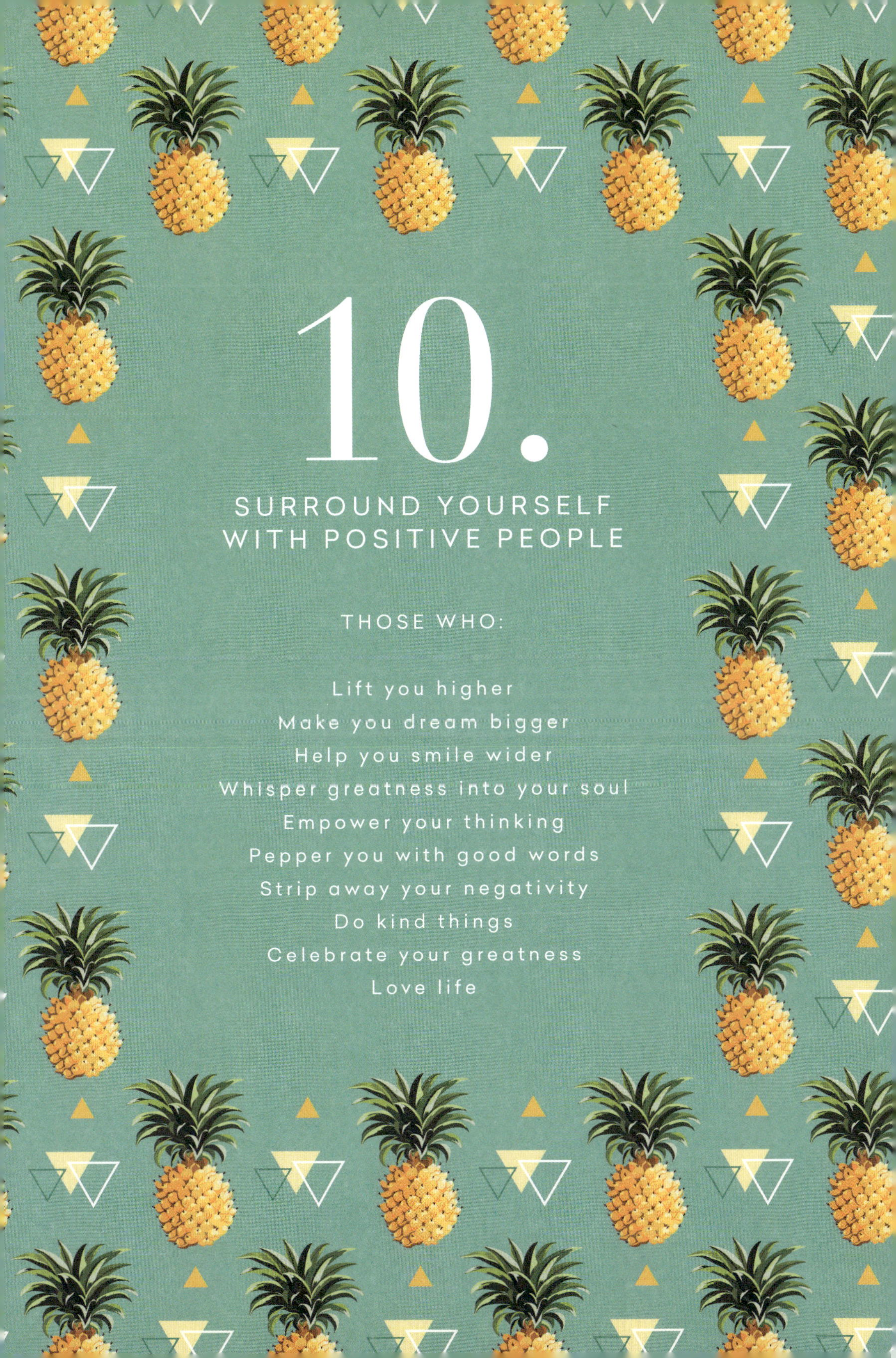

10.

SURROUND YOURSELF
WITH POSITIVE PEOPLE

THOSE WHO:

Lift you higher
Make you dream bigger
Help you smile wider
Whisper greatness into your soul
Empower your thinking
Pepper you with good words
Strip away your negativity
Do kind things
Celebrate your greatness
Love life

11.

USE MUSIC AS MEDICINE

When someone belts out exactly what you're feeling with uncanny accuracy (like Taylor Swift: "cause I knew you were trouble when you walked in"), cue the tear fest. But go on, indulge, because it can actually be good for you, something countless music studies from around the globe, conducted over many decades, have confirmed. Music can lift our mood, help us cry, comfort our sadness, trigger memories, help us reflect and cause us to be empathetic, which is brilliant when you are in the midst of break-up psychosis and lifting your gaze off yourself and onto anything around you is hard. The lyrics themselves can make you feel understood, less alone or even optimistic about tomorrow, helping you survive the day or more permanently, move on in your heart and mind. So, throw back to Sinead O'Connor's 1990s classic 'Nothing Compares 2 U' and let the tears flow. Unsure of an exact playlist? Why don't you...

TRY THIS:
♫'All Too Well' (2012) – TAYLOR SWIFT
♫'Stay With Me' (2014) – SAM SMITH
♫'Because of You' (2004) – KELLY CLARKSON
♫'I Will Always Love You' (1992) – WHITNEY HOUSTON
♫'Someone Like You' (2011) – ADELE
♫'Un-Break My Heart' (1996) – TONI BRAXTON
♫'It Must Have Been Love' (1990) – ROXETTE
♫'Total Eclipse of the Heart' (1983) – BONNIE TYLER
♫'Love the Way You Lie' (2010) – EMINEM FEAT. RIHANNA

ready for a
positive shift?

♫'Stronger' (2000) – BRITNEY SPEARS
♫'We Are Never Ever Getting Back Together'
(2012) – TAYLOR SWIFT
♫'So What' (2009) – P!NK
♫'Big Girls Don't Cry' (1962) – FRANKIE VALLI
AND THE FOUR SEASONS
♫'I Don't Need a Man' (2005) – THE PUSSYCAT DOLLS
♫'Irreplaceable' (2006) – BEYONCÉ
♫'Rolling in the Deep' (2011) – ADELE
♫'I Will Survive' (1978) – GLORIA GAYNOR
♫'You're So Vain' (1972) – CARLY SIMON
♫'Where I Stood' (2007) – MISSY HIGGINS

As the days roll by (and the tissues start running low), change the soundtrack as your mood does. Shift to music that makes you feel strong and empowered or that makes you laugh. As I write this, a Whitney Houston song just started playing on the radio. Her words as I write: "I decided long ago never to walk in anyone's shadows. If I fail, if I succeed, at least I live as I believe. No matter what they take from me, they can't take away my dignity. Because the greatest love of all is happening to me, I found the greatest love of all inside of me." In the words of Whitney, "Learning to love yourself, it is the greatest love of all! … Find your strength in love." That's love of self, not love of another – and even if you are in a relationship, this stands true!

POP!

12.

WATCH SAD MOVIES

I can almost hear you: "I need to cry less, not more!" But a recent study from The Ohio State University revealed that watching sad movies actually makes us feel – wait for it – happier. Who knew? Suddenly, all those late-night viewings of *Beaches* and *Stepmom* are starting to make sense. According to the researchers, watching tragedies onscreen helps us reflect on the good relationships in our own lives and to "count our blessings" despite the sadness the storyline makes us feel in the moment. Many could argue it's a modern-day take on the ancient Greeks, who were famous for their tragic plays offered as catharsis. Either way, indulge with two boxes of tissues in hand (one is never going to be enough) and let that increased thoughtfulness unfold so it can help your thought-life navigate through all the darkness to find a bit of light, even if it's supersonically small. Wah!

TRY THESE TEAR-JERKERS:

BEACHES (1988)

Possibly the saddest movie ever
[spoiler alert] when a best friend and mother dies.

PRECIOUS (2009)

The devastating, yet inspirational tale of overcoming tough challenges.

GHOST (1990)

Life beyond death and… *that* pottery scene!
Plus just enough Whoopi Goldberg to make you laugh.

THE NOTEBOOK (2004)

Ryan Gosling. Enough said.
(And war and heartbreak and kissing in the rain.)

ATONEMENT (2007)

Two lovers separated by war and injustice.

I AM SAM (2001)

The beautiful tale of a father-daughter relationship when
the father has a developmental disorder.

SCHINDLER'S LIST (1993)

A gripping World War II film.

MARLEY & ME (2008)

The beautiful (and real) tale of how life unfolds around our pets.

TITANIC (1997)

"I will never let go, Jack. I will never let go…"

THE FAULT IN OUR STARS (2014)

Falling in love when it's complicated.

(Closely followed by the 2002 drama *A Walk To Remember*)

HOTEL RWANDA (2004)

This may make you more angry than sad, but a tear-jerker

(and important story) all the same.

BAMBI (1942), E.T. THE EXTRA-TERRESTRIAL (1982), UP (2009)

Who said these were just for kids?

THE INTOUCHABLES (2011)

An unlikely friendship between a wealthy quadriplegic

and his caretaker, a former inmate.

IT'S A WONDERFUL LIFE (1946)

A classic reminder that everyone is special,

even when we don't feel like we are.

13.

ACT WITH DIGNITY AND GRACE

A friend who had been through a painful divorce gave me some frank, wise advice on this subject and it went like this:

"He'll be a dickhead and you'll want to be a bitch. But just don't."

It was brutal, funny and true all in one. The truth is, in most cases you are both hurting, even if it's for very different reasons. And oh my, did I want to scream and rant and throw his clothes on the pavement and send horrendous text messages and post my (not so great) thoughts on social media at times? YES. I. DID. But, I purposefully and specifically chose not to. Not once. It was possibly the hardest thing I've ever had to do, to exhibit so much restraint. Looking back, I couldn't be prouder of myself and I put it down to this small sentence that became a personal mantra: "Act with dignity and grace." In previous relationships, I hadn't been so in control and later regretted it.

There is the old saying, "What you say about someone else actually says more about you than them," and it still rings true today. You certainly cannot control the other person, but you can control yourself. I found in doing so, you're not letting them off the hook so much (I did ponder this thought at times), but strengthening your own sense of self and sharpening your character.

This can be excruciatingly – somebody-take-my-iPhone-away-from-me-right-NOW – hard, but it's not just them, you have yourself to think about; how exercising restraint will make you feel in the long run. Acting with dignity and grace will help you to stay powerfully in your centre, which will allow you to move forward in the most positive, gentle and loving way.

When it gets so difficult that you feel the pressure valves starting to pop, remind yourself of the principles of karma (skip to Step 21 for more on this), close your eyes, take six deep breaths and know you are rising above the situation – say a meditation mantra if you have one, or even roll the wise words from my friend around in your head until you feel on top of the situation. There will be moments when you lose it, but don't beat yourself up. You're doing great by considering and attempting an alternative route to trashing them privately or publicly, and it gets easier as you go along.

I've found that the busier I get, the calmer I get (I don't know how this happens, but it does and it has to!). I managed to somehow maintain this around the break-up – the more my ex baited me and attempted to reconnect, the calmer, more graceful and dignified I somehow became. And with this came a great sense of personal peace.

Resist the instant gratification of hurling insults and getting things off your chest, and it will pay off. Every. Single. Time. If Bridget Jones could do it in a kinky bunny outfit (when she found a naked woman in her boyfriend's bathtub), you can too.

close
your
EYES AND
take six
deep
BREATHS.

acceptance

14.
BE GRATEFUL

REMEMBER
that sometimes
not getting
what you want
is a WONDERFUL
stroke of luck.
– ANONYMOUS

LOVE

15.

EXPRESS YOURSELF

A break-up hurtles you into a head spin. You'll have a million thoughts – most of them negative – and unfortunately our minds don't come with a built-in filing system to organise or keep them locked away. They can (and do) spring up at any (and every) second! Not a big journaller? You might change your mind when you realise what a tangled mess you have going on upstairs.

Writing about stressors or traumatic events has been linked to both psychological and physiological health, including decreases in both distress and depression and even positive changes in the immune system (which is super handy if you've been digging into piles of comfort food). And it really doesn't need to be a novel. Gretchen Rubin, author of *The Happiness Project*, speaks about the benefits of keeping a single-sentence journal.

"One sentence is enough," she says in a podcast. "When I look back on it years later, the one sentence really does keep memories valid." And while you might think you won't want to remember what you're going through now, Gretchen assures us that "we tend to write down the happier things", meaning this brief moment of self-reflection could in fact help nurture a more positive attitude.

Personally, I write exactly what I'm feeling and it tends to be more negative than positive – I write it and rarely look at it again. It allows me to get those emotions out so they don't keep swimming around in my head. There will always be a unique approach that works for you – it could be happy, it could be sad, it could be long, it could be short, and all are okay.

More of a typist than a writer? There are a ton of journalling services that are nice and simple, like myeveningpost.com. It sends you an email every night, you reply about your day and then sit back and watch your online diary grow. I promise, it will get brighter day by day.

UNSURE WHERE TO START? THESE TIPS MIGHT HELP:

Try answering these three questions:
1. What was terrible about today?
2. What was great about today?
3. How do I want to change tomorrow?

If that's too tough, go for the abstract with these:
1. If I was a fruit today, I would have been…
2. If I was a colour today, I would have been…
3. The first five words that come to my mind are:

Don't overthink it. Write whatever comes to mind, don't stop yourself because you think it's wrong, mean, rude or politically incorrect (you can always burn it later!). If you can't keep up with the speed of your subconscious flow, type instead.

i write because i don't know what i think until i read what i say.

don't cry
because it's over,
SMILE
because it
happened.
- ANONYMOUS

16.

CHOOSE TO GROW

Sometimes it's only when we hit rock bottom that we're forced to reach into the deepest reserves of our soul in order to find the strength to lift ourselves back up. And often, we find ourselves stretched and expanded as we reach around, hunting for the magic that will get us through.

While you're shedding tears and devouring salted caramel gelato on the couch, thank the universe because behind the scenes, your survival instincts are kicking in, revving up to expand you beyond where you thought possible in your previously cosy, coupled-up life.

Just for a second, think about your relationship towards the end and get honest with yourself – can you say it was expansive and progressing, or was it more stagnant, stuck or regressing? In most cases, it was some form of the latter – and it makes sense because there's a rule in nature that if things aren't growing, they're dying. It is the perfect rationale for culling dead leaves and replacing them with shiny new shoots.

The very fact that your relationship has ended means that the energetic frequency of either you or your former partner – or both – had changed. There's no going back, so go forwards instead with the enormous power that only being brought to your knees can produce. Now is the time to launch yourself to heights you've never imagined (or you have imagined, but were never going to reach for within the comfortable box of your relationship).

Give your spirit free rein to soar. Practically, that can mean doing things or going places you have dreamed of, but at a deeper level, there are many qualities (think courage, independence and a glass-half-full mentality) you'll likely have to draw on to get through the aftermath of a pummelled heart – and out the other side. As a bonus, just like the self-love muscle, the more you work these qualities now, the stronger they'll remain once your heart has healed.

If your energy has changed so much that your former relationship is no longer on your wavelength, just imagine the relationship possibilities that will be drawn to this new wavelength – not to mention all the other life opportunities awaiting you.

It's from this space that you can find a sense of gratitude for the whole, messy experience (you might not be feeling that just yet, but it will come). Your break-up doesn't have to leave you broken – in fact, once you've put yourself back together again, you'll likely find that the sum of the parts now equals way, way more than the previous whole. Allow yourself that tub of salted caramel gelato in the meantime.

17.

BE YOUR OWN THERAPIST

On those days where your mind is going rampant with 'what ifs' and generally scary thoughts around your break-up ("They said X, so they must never have really loved me," or "There's a pic of them partying on Facebook… instead of mourning our break-up, they're celebrating!"), do a little CBT (cognitive behavioural therapy) on yourself to flip negative/hurtful thinking on its head. Your thoughts have a huge power over your emotions and how you feel in each moment. Whether you're conscious of it or not, each less-than-sunny thought is basically the equivalent of shooting an emotional dagger into your heart. So, it's worth trying this technique recommended by renowned motivational speaker and life coach Tony Robbins: whenever you find yourself sinking into a mental rut, ask yourself, "What else could this mean?" In this way, "I'll never find anyone else" becomes, "I'm being set free to find my real soul mate."

It's worth taking a little detour here to note that thinking positive is not an excuse to go into denial mode. Convincing yourself that your ex has stopped participating in your 'seeking closure' text rally because they're penning a long 'I want you back' letter will only send you two steps backwards. The key when working on your mindset is to get a more rational perspective – and that means looking forward, not back.

After all, there's only so long that your best mates will play amateur counsellor before you need to take control yourself. So, if you find that your self-talk has turned into a constant stream of negativity, start playing watchdog over your thoughts and commit to observing your mindset throughout the day. Each time you find yourself thinking something negative in regards to your break-up, stop your mind in its tracks and replace the thought with something more helpful. Even if you only catch 10 per cent of your dark thoughts to start with, training your brain is just like flexing your muscles at the gym – you'll get stronger and more capable every day.

They say that whatever you believe, is true for you – so instead of waking up to a reality that's filled with doom and darkness, why not help yourself through this emotionally draining time by creating an outlook that is as beautiful and comforting as possible?

And if it all gets too much, be smart and seek a professional early. Sometimes you can't do it on your own and you need a professional to help you find a way through the fog; they can help you know what 'work' is necessary and how to do it. Don't resist seeking expert therapy – there's no shame in asking for help, in fact, it's a sign of self-awareness and wisdom, in my opinion.

I AM
beautiful

I AM kind
I AM capable
I AM enough

18.

BOOST YOUR SELF-LOVE

When you've got a plus-one, it's practically an unwritten agreement that they'll have your back. At. All. Times. In a relationship (at least while the going's still good), your other half can become your number one cheerleader – that source of endless love to bolster you up when you've had a bad day, if there's trouble at work or if you find yourself in a mid-life, quarter-life, anytime-of-life crisis. That makes separation one of the hardest things, because they also take with them that constant source of love and support. Especially as some people, over the course of a love story, can find themselves coming to enjoy – and even rely on – this on-tap TLC so much that they disconnect from their own self-love over time.

This whole scenario is mightily inconvenient after a break-up, because when your ex implements their exit strategy, that's exactly when your sorrowful heart and battered self-esteem are most thirsty for a love top-up. Whether you have disconnected from your own self-love or not, you can never be too kind to your soul. I believe – and I am sure you know what I'm going to say here – that after a break-up, you have to be your own Prince Charming and come to your own rescue by flexing that self-love muscle.

For some of us, the concept of self-love can seem downright weird at first. I'm not talking about shouting "I'm amazing and I rule the world" from the rooftops (although that does help some people and you can also do that if you please – my neighbour does, actually!). It's mainly about taking care of yourself during the 'blah' days, replacing those self-harming (and downright mean) thoughts or soul-destroying, self-directed judgements with kinder self-talk and acceptance of all the beautiful facets of yourself.

If you're thinking things such as "I'm not good enough for him or her" or "there must be something wrong with me" after the break-up, your need to nurture your wounded heart is absolutely magnified. This can be as simple as taking yourself off for a mini-pedicure on a Sunday morning (instead of lamenting how this is normally when you and your ex would be heading for breakfast at your favourite cafe... and they'd be ordering this… and you'd be joking together about that…) or ensuring you have a plus-one all ready to go for the next work function.

It can mean saying 'no' to social requests that you would normally feel an obligation to attend, giving yourself a free pass because you know that for now, it will hurt. It can mean revelling in the financial freedom to buy yourself flowers each week if they bring you joy, or indulging in a massage more often than you normally would to feel special and relaxed.

Little acts of self-love can give you regular reminders that you are still special and amazing. And after a while, you will start to feel that way again (you may just need to give yourself a little nudge). Even if you're way off thinking about moving on at this stage, just know when you fill yourself up with love from the inside out, this is when you'll most powerfully attract new love into your life.

Another way to beat this truth back into your brain after a break-up is to use mantras. A mantra is simply a combination of words that you repeat in your head – it could be during your meditation, while on your morning walk or in the car to work. You could try saying, "I love and accept all parts of myself" or "I am enough" or "I am a good person".

Or, when you wake up in the morning and you head straight to your bathroom, instead of passing the mirror and thinking, "Ugh, look at those bags under my eyes," try stopping, looking straight into your eyes and saying, "I love you, thanks for letting me see the world." Yep, it might feel pretty confronting or strange at first, but do it anyway – I dare you – and watch how healthy it is for your mind and soul over time.

LOOKING FOR THE RIGHT MANTRA
FOR YOU? TRY ONE OF THESE:

I accept myself for who I am

I am living in this moment –
and it's wonderful, even when it hurts

I am in the right place in my life, right now

I have everything I need

I am not alone

I am loved and will let love in

I am grateful

I am beauty in this world

I respect myself

I believe in myself

I deserve happiness and release personal fear

I know I can be a world changer

I know I have a purpose

I deserve to dream

I choose to be confident

I choose to have an open mind

I choose to be mindful in everything I do

When my heart was most fragile, my
good friend Bradley Trevor Greive
penned these words for me:

rest assured you are
still composed of
the same matter as
the brightest stars
in the universe.
you may feel a
little crushed and
dimmed by what has
happened, but...

YOU WILL
light up the sky
because that is
WHO YOU ARE.

19.

CLOSE THE DOOR
WITHOUT CLOSURE

If we had our way, we'd square everything off in life perfectly, like reading the final pages of a book and putting it back on the bookshelf before we start a new one. If only life was that neat and tidy. Geez, sometimes you don't even get halfway through the book and it's gone. You might make it to the final chapter, only for the ink to be blurred or pages to be missing. Sometimes you lose the book altogether… and you never ever know what happened in the end.

But in reality, says Nancy Berns, author of *Closure: The Rush to End Grief and What It Costs Us*, closure is not what we really need. She suggests we close the door – without closure.

"After a break-up, people often wonder, 'Do I need closure?' No, you do not need closure… closure is not some naturally occurring emotion that we can simply find with the right advice. Healing? Yes, healing is possible, but that is different from closure," wrote Nancy for *Psychology Today*.

We all want to know why. Most of the time this longing for closure is disguised as a need for validation, vindication or justification. Ultimately, what's more important – and helpful – to know is that someone's 'truth' about the 'why' is just their version – their truth. We are all just extras in someone else's movie. What a 'failed' relationship really comes down to isn't actually personal – even though it damn well feels personal at the time!

The cold hard truth is that closure is just a myth, and a recipe for misery if you try and chase it by re-opening lines of communication and old wounds with your ex. That 'last relationship talk' (or shag… for that matter) won't leave you feeling enlightened or empowered – it'll leave you hurting, confused and angry. Again.

Closure won't come by making your ex jealous, proving you're better off without them or relinquishing them of the 'power'. In fact, it has nothing to do with them at all. Others can't give you your neat and finite 'finish'; it only comes when you decide it has.

So, forget closure. Just close the door gently (or slam it – whatever feels best) and move on. New adventures are waiting for you…

20.

LET GO OF YOUR EGO

Warning: this step will sting, but it will be worth it.

More often than not, the pain or anger at the end of a relationship can have more to do with a hurt ego than anything else. And at times, it can be ego that got us here in the first place. It is a wild beast. It can be mean, ugly, stubborn and controlling, but it can also grow and shrink with the power we give it. What is ego? It's said to be "the part of the mind that mediates between the conscious and the unconscious and is responsible for reality testing and a sense of personal identity".

There's the motivational quote, which flies around the Internet with warp speed at least once a year: "Ego – three little letters that keep us from saying things we really need to say like: 'I love you, I miss you and I'm sorry'." Yep, you got it.

So often the 'hurt' isn't actually caused by a loss of love, but rather a bruising (or bashing) of ego; ego that thought no one in a sane state would let you get away! And that's a fair point, surely! There's also the uglier side of ego, with thoughts of, "I am better than you", "I am better than this", "I deserve more" or "I am above this". Ego can be accusatory in its manifestation to say, "I would never have done that", "How could you do this to me?" or "You should say sorry to ME!" and then it's a rapid descent into destruction if either party won't back down.

But back to your bruised post-break-up ego… The best way to get through this is to acknowledge that we all have ego, that it can be toxic to who we are, debilitating to our future and that it isn't a measurement of truth. Then you will be ready to let it go.

TRY THESE THREE APPROACHES:

1. FEEL THE LOVE

"Whenever you're afraid, it's proof that you've turned your back on love and chosen to have faith in the ego." So says Gabrielle Bernstein, who firmly believes that love is the only emotion that really exists. Take a leaf out of this spirit junkie's book and as soon as you're feeling anxious or fearful, say to yourself, "Love did not create this thought, and so it is not real." Even if you don't quite believe it (trust me, I know how nutty it might sound), you'll be amazed how this simple mantra can change your perspective and derail negative thoughts.

starve
your ego.
feed
your soul.

– ANONYMOUS

2. QUASH THE NEED TO WIN

Marianne Williamson (who beautifully endorsed another of my books, *Money
& Mindfulness: Living in Abundance*), puts it like this: "The ego says, 'Once
everything falls into place, I'll feel peace.' The spirit says, 'Find your peace, and
then everything will fall into place.'" If you're as competitive as I am, this one's
hard to crack. What you need to remember is that striving to win at everything is
not only fruitless (and in today's endless rat race, absolutely impossible!), but also
just a way to avoid checking in with your true self. You can't win all of the time,
and when a relationship breaks down, there are no winners. There's nothing to be
gained from plotting to out-do your ex – just by putting your energy towards this,
you've already lost. Let go of the need for recognition and set yourself free.

3. BE GRATEFUL

According to Deepak Chopra, "Even in turning to ourselves we must go beyond
the constant clamour of ego, beyond the tools of logic and reason, to the still,
calm place within us: the realm of the soul." In the midst of a break-up, you might
not feel particularly grateful, especially with feelings like anger to contend with.
This is normal – it's your ego defending itself. But think outside of your current
circumstances and focus on the other parts of your life. Make a list. Even if you
can only think of one thing to be grateful for (is it sunny outside today? There
you go!), write it down and really be grateful for it. Think about your family,
friends, pets, health, job, passions… all of the things outside of your relationship
that define you, and add them to the list. Did you do your laundry today? On the
list! Even this small step is a leap in the right direction.

                       BREAK-UPS & BREAKTHROUGHS

21.
TRUST IN KARMA

There are many ways to look at karma but I love this common explanation that karma is when an action, either born of love or fear, is revisited upon someone at a later date. It wasn't too long ago that this concept was passed off as hippie talk, rejected by the mainstream, something for those who wear tie-dye and smoke things they really shouldn't. But it's a mainstay in today's world, a household concept from East to West with the topic discussed, embraced and even manifested en masse. Let's face it, there is comfort in believing you will eventually brandish the upper hand when you feel you have been wronged in a situation.

You might have heard the saying, "Anger is like drinking poison and expecting the other person to die," – and so it goes that having faith in karma will be infinitely more helpful if you focus less on wishing the universe would send your ex karma in the form of job loss/flesh-eating disease/some other equally hideous fate, and more on upping your own karma bank balance via phenomenal things to come.

Either way, it's a great comfort post break-up. You really do have to trust the unseen process and just walk away when all you want to do (we all feel like this at one point) is slash their car tyres or at the very least, send them mean texts. It is said, "Karma's a bitch!" and yes, that's true, but I think karma can also be an angel. Most times, you won't see karma in action and you'll just have to trust that a greater good has seen justice done.

Have you ever been in puddles of tears after being knocked back for a job you'd had your whole heart set on, only to be offered another role a few months later that's a thousand times more right for you? We don't always know what's best for us at the time, but we have to trust that the universe does.

Your break-up doesn't equal the end of the story – it's merely the conclusion of this particular chapter, and you just never know what is to come.

     BREAK-UPS & BREAKTHROUGHS

what goes around comes back ... going again around

let it be
22.
SURRENDER

As spiritual teacher Marianne Williamson says, "Something amazing happens when we surrender and just love. We melt into another world, a realm of power already within us. The world changes when we change. The world softens when we soften. The world loves us when we choose to love the world."

Surrender has a lot to do with closure, and being okay with not getting any.

You'll never be able to understand everything, and you actually don't need to.

You can't win every battle, and you shouldn't expect to.

There won't be an answer to everything, and that's okay.

So, what is a broken soul to do? You can fight, protest, shout and demand or you can accept and surrender, which will ultimately bring you peace. Sometimes you need to fight, but other times you need to look back and say "what's done is done", and see that each day is the chance for a new beginning.

The key to acceptance is to relinquish control. I find the serenity prayer immensely helpful for this. If you don't believe in God or a higher power, there is still great power in this prayer:

"God, grant me the serenity to accept the things I cannot change, the courage to change the things I can, and the wisdom to know the difference."

Light a candle, take a bath, breathe deeply and let it go. Detachment from outcome is one of the most powerful things you can practise.

23.
BELIEVE IN A POWER
GREATER THAN YOU

And I'm not talking about the government here! It could be God, Buddha, angels, the universe, an energy or just a feeling that there is something greater guiding you and looking after you.

I realise this is a deeply personal decision, one that can be polarising and something that can take moments or years to explore. However, this has been a huge source of strength for me at many times in my life and for that reason, I want to share it with you.

In the moments when you feel almost unbearably alone, believing in a greater power and trusting that they 'have your back' can bring you some much-needed reassurance and spiritual strength, which ultimately can lead to greater peace of mind, understanding and acceptance. I don't think it makes you weak, naive or unintelligent to do so, quite the contrary – you feel empowered and almost supercharged. Why not explore and choose for yourself?

Go to church, visit a temple, speak to a monk – however it best works for you – so you are uplifted, warmed, loved, filled with peace and assurance beyond what you can produce on your own. I truly believe that if you look for extra support, you will find it.

We don't need to walk around on this planet thinking we are completely alone or that we have to carry everything on our own – that is a horrible place to rest. It is okay to be an intelligent human being and still acknowledge that you are not in control of everything, even if you haven't worked out exactly who or what is.

24.

NO 'IF ONLYS'

"If only they'd change"; "If only I had a better job"; "If only I'd given them one more chance"… The nagging, self-blaming 'if only' phase of a break-up can hold you back and keep you in the past. It's natural to look over your shoulder, re-hash and theorise about how you could have done things differently, but here's a simple truth to consider: IT IS DONE.

Surely, you did everything in your power to make it work, and that means no amount of flailing about over imaginary outcomes is going to serve you now. Perhaps you should re-read that sentence and repeat this to yourself, "Surely, I did everything I could, in my power, to make it work." Read it again if you're still struggling to digest it.

Then… agree to accept it for what it is and move on. It takes a strong mind to read that and then put it into practice, but if you can muster up the discipline and mental strength to snap off negative thinking and mentally move on, you will be empowered.

While thinking that you could have done things differently can help you be a better person in future relationships, it can be destructive to you in this moment. It can trap you in a victim mentality and stop you from the necessary actions or new decisions to move you forward and help you create the life you need and the life you deserve.

LIFE is too short to worry about TODAY'S mistake. because there is TOMORROW.

IF YOU ARE STRUGGLING WITH 'IF ONLYS',
TRY THIS QUICK, POWERFUL EXERCISE:

1. GET ALL OF YOUR 'IF ONLYS' OUT.
That's right, list them. Every single one you can think of.

2. BIN THE LIST. Or even burn it if that will be more powerful.
I am a big believer in the significance of rituals and physical demonstrations
to the outside world of what we are declaring on the inside.

If only I hadn't said… If only I had said… If only I'd been more…
If only I'd been less… If only they knew… If only I knew…
If only we could… If only I could… If only they could…
If only… If only… If only… If only… If only… If only…

Time to bury or burn… and re-emerge without regret.

25.
ACKNOWLEDGE
LIFE HAS SEASONS

seasons change, just like winter turns into spring. never fight it.

keep your eyes wide for change on the horizon and embrace it.

— LISA MESSENGER

26.

RECLAIM YOUR WEEKENDS

Sooooo much free time on your hands? It's amazing how much time that relationship chewed up – thank goodness it's over. Too soon to joke about it? Ok, got it… Ending a relationship can often result in you having a LOT more free time than you used to. If you're working or studying, weekdays range from pleasantly full to manic – consumed by running to meetings, slotting in the gym, making lunches, grabbing a mid-week movie, picking up the dry cleaning and generally keeping everything in your world all harmoniously spinning (and this isn't even factoring in kids if you have them). We are the masters of the full mid-week life, which is definitely compounded when you are in love and have two schedules to organise like a game of Tetris. But when 9am rolls around on a Saturday morning after your break-up (or 5.58am for the parents), the whirl of the weekday rush can stop in a single, deafening moment. Silence. A tumbleweed rolls by your phone. There is no lazy brunch, market crawl or mountainous adventure planned for you today. Suddenly, you notice every happy couple passing by with their tennis rackets, hiking boots, yoga mats or concert tickets in hand, en route to a perfect 48 hours of weekend bliss. Tick, tick, tick. You're still at home, alone.

It will pass, but those early post-relationship days can be a lonesome time. One of the best things you can do is reclaim those weekends for *you* and fill them with all the adventures, hobbies or stillness that either got lost in the midst of your relationship or was scaled back because of other priorities. Whatever the case, you have an incredible reason to throw yourself into life in a fun, recreational way, which will make your heart smile and potentially, your muscles hurt. Unsure where to go from here?

TRY THESE IDEAS TO GET YOU MOVING:

GET UP

Snoozing for longer than an hour over your weekday rise-and-shine time on the weekend can knock your circadian rhythm out of whack, so try and keep your sleeping routine in check.

START THAT HOBBY

The one you have been putting off for months (okay, years). Learn a new language, become a mountain climber, try ocean swimming, take up tae kwon do, decorate cakes, join a chess club, go to a book club, learn how to sculpt ice, get your scuba diving certificate, find a pen friend, volunteer at a community group, join the theatre, learn to fly a plane, start guitar lessons, start a food blog… It's also a great opportunity to meet new people – people who don't know your story or your ex so you are free to chat about everything else, or free to dish some dirt and then move on. (Go to step 35 for more on hobbies.)

KICK-START HEALTHY HABITS

Perhaps you want to get back into hip-hop yoga or shopping for organic fruit and veg at the markets. Whatever your personal health goals, the weekend is the perfect time to get them up and rolling.

DO FREE STUFF

Everyone loves a bargain and utilising free things in your town or city often forces you to go to places, do things and meet people you wouldn't normally. Join the library, visit art galleries and museums, find community fairs, go to pop-up concerts, tour old buildings… Cities are generally more blessed in this area than regional locations but it's not impossible – be willing to travel and stay extra open-minded to try whatever is on offer.

today is an ADVENTURE kind of day.

INCLUDE ADVENTURE

There's security in routine and as we age, research says we like to assert more control over everything. So, say no to convention by continually adding adventure to your everyday. It pushes and stretches your mind and body, but also gets the endorphins flowing and your excitement levels soaring. Do big things, like skydiving or leaving work on a Friday and spontaneously travelling somewhere for the weekend instead of going home, right through to small yet disruptive things, like trying a new (and challenging) gym class, skinny-dipping or eating snails for the first time. And... would it kill you to wear prints?

NURTURE YOURSELF

Bake a cake or become a green thumb, both are nurturing activities for your mind, often resulting in clarity and perspective, even if you are simply tending to a houseplant. And if you try the former, there will be cake. Do you need another reason?

GET (OR BORROW) A PET

Weekends are always better with a furry friend, from evenings snuggling on the couch to fast-paced walks on the beach. If you haven't got one of your own, offer to walk your friend or neighbour's dog, or put your hand up to cat-sit.

IMMERSE YOURSELF IN CULTURE AND TRIBES

Supermarkets aren't the most inspiring places to spend your weekend, so seek out and trawl through a local farmers' or craft market and chat to the very people who grew the potatoes you are about to eat.

Visit multicultural suburbs for a food crawl (traditional pho, anyone?) and plenty of people watching, or do something with a crowd like an outdoor movie or charity run.

TAKE UP A CAUSE

Volunteer at the local zoo or community garden, offer your incredible weekday skills to a non-profit, teach refugees English, pour soup for the homeless, teach art to kids from disadvantaged backgrounds, sing to old people, dress up as a clown for unwell babies.

EXPAND YOUR MIND

Get lost in Wikipedia, take a new course, host a board game night (think Cards Against Humanity), read a new genre, randomly buy theatre tickets, write.

GET A (FUN) SECOND JOB

Make ice-cream, walk dogs, (legally) graffiti walls, taste-test hot dogs, shadow a chocolatier, take city tours, be a personal shopper, teach yoga, become a wedding planner or wildlife rehabilitator.

EXPLORE

Get in your car or jump on a train or bus and go bush, beach or mountain-top for the day. Even a mini getaway can lower stress and make you feel better all over.

Then... when everyone asks you what you did this past weekend, you'll have a cracking answer.

27.

DON'T GO BACK, GO FORWARD

In the haze of early break-up days (and the face of completely irrational fears of being alone forever) your ex can look really appealing! And if you were very much in love at the time of your break-up, or there are other people involved (namely smaller peeps), or extra complications to consider (like houses, loans and pre-paid holidays), you could be tempted to sprint back into their arms.

Yet, while things may have changed between you since the break-up and there might be some water under the bridge by now (more than a third of cohabitating couples and one-fifth of couples who are now hitched have actually broken up at some point in the past, so says a study from Kansas State University), I'm going to go with the odds and err on the side of things being squarely as they were. If that is the case for you, let me say…

HOME TRUTH #1
It is a bad idea to go back there.

HOME TRUTH #2
It will most likely end in more heartache (research confirms it).

HOME TRUTH #3
Chances are, you'll be even more broken than you are now.

Initially, it's all too easy to dream about magically reconciling your differences, but consider this: a survey out of the University of Texas found more than 60 per cent of young adults have gone back to their ex at least once. Of these couples, three-quarters break up and make up again (and in many cases… again after that!). As tempting as an on-again-off-again ride may sound (remind me, why do we do it to ourselves?), wouldn't you rather invest that time in yourself and in

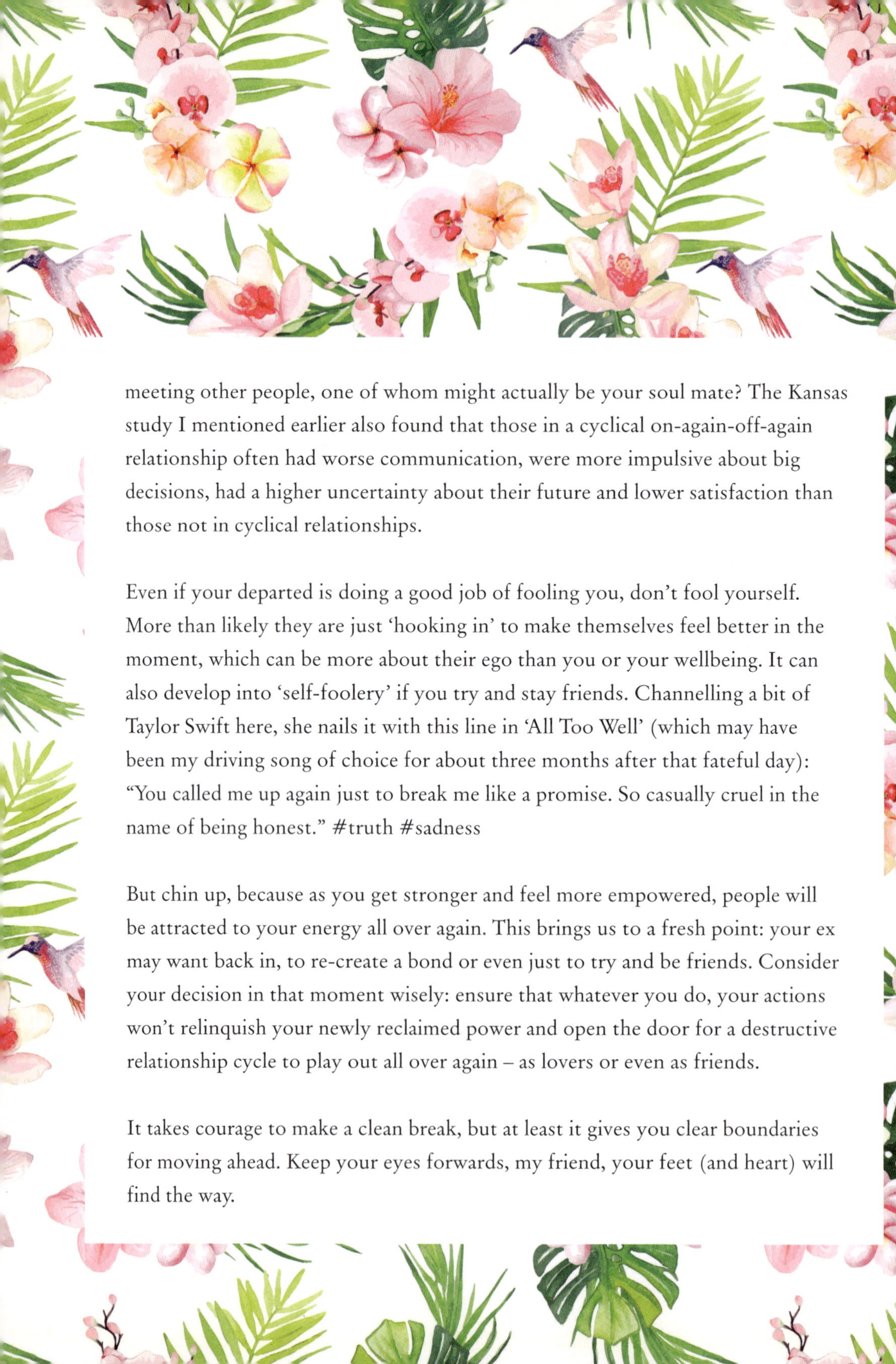

meeting other people, one of whom might actually be your soul mate? The Kansas study I mentioned earlier also found that those in a cyclical on-again-off-again relationship often had worse communication, were more impulsive about big decisions, had a higher uncertainty about their future and lower satisfaction than those not in cyclical relationships.

Even if your departed is doing a good job of fooling you, don't fool yourself. More than likely they are just 'hooking in' to make themselves feel better in the moment, which can be more about their ego than you or your wellbeing. It can also develop into 'self-foolery' if you try and stay friends. Channelling a bit of Taylor Swift here, she nails it with this line in 'All Too Well' (which may have been my driving song of choice for about three months after that fateful day): "You called me up again just to break me like a promise. So casually cruel in the name of being honest." #truth #sadness

But chin up, because as you get stronger and feel more empowered, people will be attracted to your energy all over again. This brings us to a fresh point: your ex may want back in, to re-create a bond or even just to try and be friends. Consider your decision in that moment wisely: ensure that whatever you do, your actions won't relinquish your newly reclaimed power and open the door for a destructive relationship cycle to play out all over again – as lovers or even as friends.

It takes courage to make a clean break, but at least it gives you clear boundaries for moving ahead. Keep your eyes forwards, my friend, your feet (and heart) will find the way.

NEVER look back. you're not going that way.

MUNCH ON THIS:

By all means be kind, complimentary and respectful to your ex, but don't forget who they have shown themselves to be when things really mattered. As a dear friend said to me in the days after my break-up: "Ex-lovers all come crawling back eventually, sometimes more than once, but don't weaken because you miss being with them when they were at their best. Keep your true friends close as you'll need their support to avoid poor choices. You can certainly forgive mistakes, but you cannot forgive bad faith. Disagreements are one thing, failing the foxhole test is another; you must stay strong and know that you can and will do better – because you will."

28.

FORGIVE YOURSELF

No one's asking you to forgive them – just yet – but there is one person you MUST forgive: yourself.

Don't be angry, ashamed or embarrassed that you didn't see this coming. Don't crucify yourself for not listening to the warnings of others (if they existed) or the inklings you may have felt deep down. Don't suggest to your soul that you should have been more discerning, to your mind that you should have been smarter or to your heart that it should have been less vulnerable.

You fell in love and you had your heart broken. The end.

It's an easy trap to fall into and an abyss you can be lost in for weeks (even months), but the sooner you let yourself off the hook, the sooner you will truly be free of this. I am speaking from experience. I was incredibly hard on myself, if only for a short period. I do believe that everything happens for a reason, and therefore, I was able to powerfully move myself out of a dark place. But while I was still very much in there, the profound words of a wise friend popped into my inbox and reached into the depths of my heart as if the universe knew I was crying out for them. The email said: "Good on you for believing in love and for having the courage to follow your heart. What a wonderful mistake to have made. You enjoyed some special moments and will be wiser for this experience, and when radiant true love comes your way, you will be able to see it for all that it is."

you
fell in
LOVE
and had
your heart
broken.
the end.

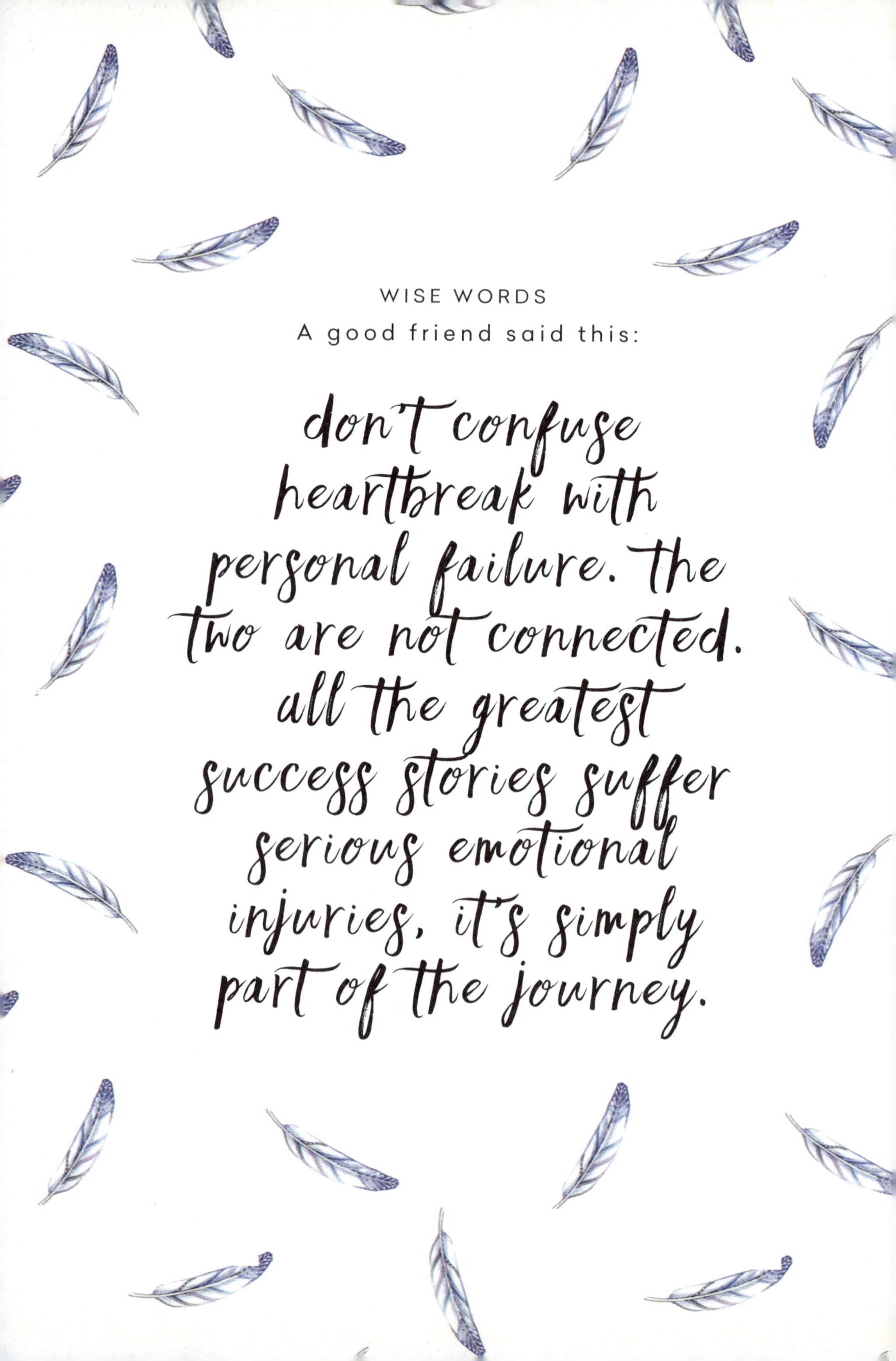

WISE WORDS
A good friend said this:

don't confuse heartbreak with personal failure. the two are not connected. all the greatest success stories suffer serious emotional injuries, it's simply part of the journey.

nourishment

29.

MEDITATE

Did you know the average person has between 50,000 and 70,000 thoughts a day? I am a big meditator and have been doing it in some form or another for 11 years. I really believe that having a stillness of mind is key to happiness and success, and that it's an amazing tool to help get you through tough times.

Meditation is all about focusing your mind enough so that you can wrangle some sort of control over it – because if your mind is all over the place, you can expect your emotions to be, too. If right now your brain is constantly whirring between something along the lines of "I miss them/I wish we'd never met/I feel so horrible" on repeat, meditation will help you find some sort of peaceful space in between the painful thoughts.

Yes, sitting down in a quiet spot with nothing but your thoughts for company (and no distractions) can be tough, especially when you're having an 'I-really-can't-adult-today-please-don't-make-me-adult-today' day. But here's the thing. You CAN do it!

The surest way to find peace and strength is to take positive steps, even if that means faking it till you make it. Meditation takes constant practice – like any muscle, regular repetitive exercise builds strength.

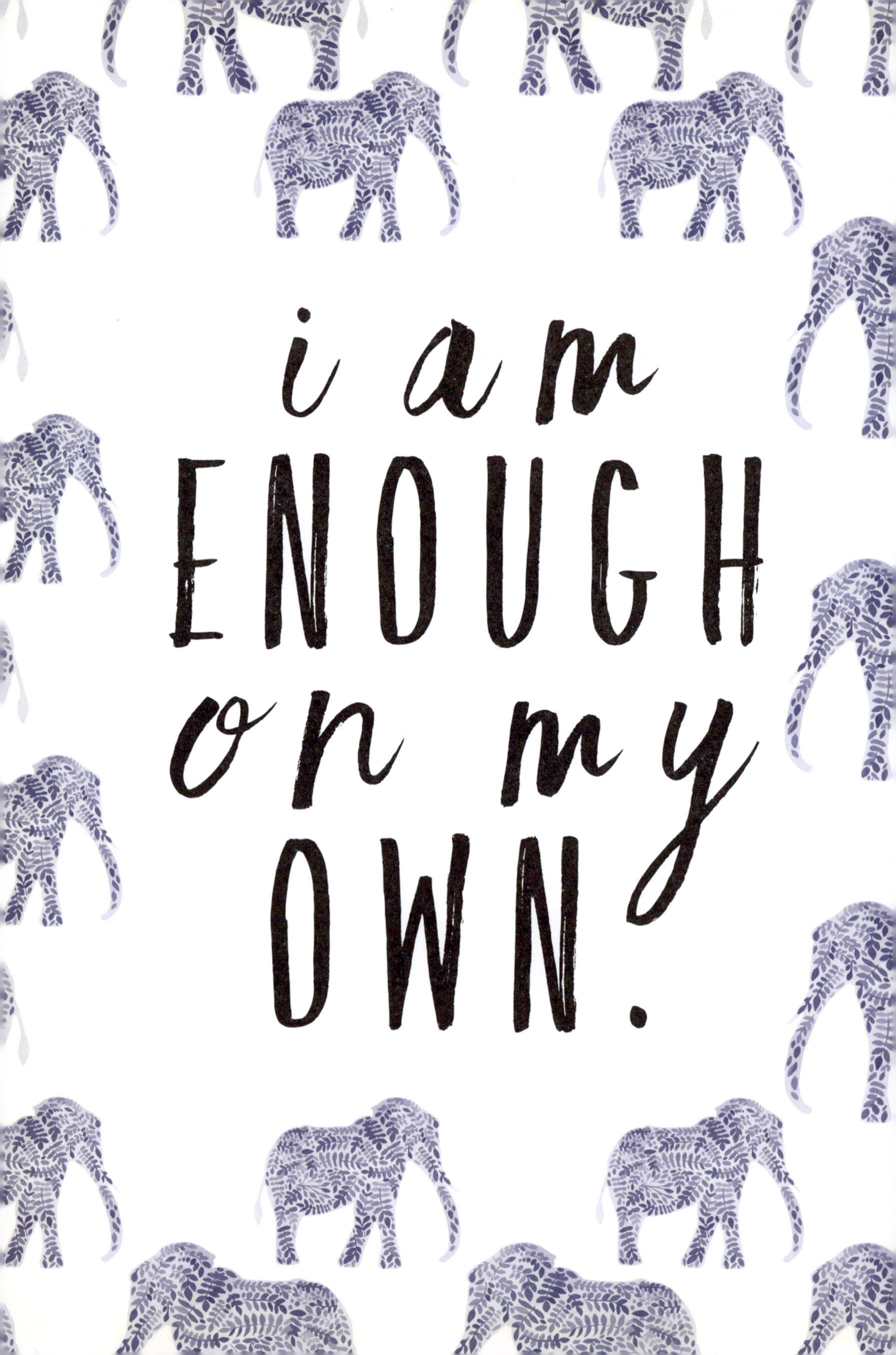

i am
ENOUGH
on my
OWN.

There are so many different meditation practices out there, so you're guaranteed to find something that works for you. Guided meditations and relaxations are wonderful when stillness is what you need, and they can lead you on powerful journeys that create deep energy shifts. Or, if you want to try something simple that you can do anywhere, try using a healing mantra as the focal point of your meditation – something like, "I am enough on my own", "I am strong enough to handle this break-up" or "I have all the love I need already within myself", whatever resonates with you.

Some of my favourites are called 'meditation burns', which are basically dance meditations. They get your energy and your body moving – and it's hard to stay sad and depressed when you've had such a great workout for body, mind and soul!

If life is busy and you're finding it hard to fit meditation in, consider this: we each have 72 lots of 20-minute blocks available to us every single day (and no doubt a few more of those are freed up now your ex is no longer taking up all that time in your life!). Surely it's possible to allocate one or two of those blocks to meditation, right?

Meditate your fear, anger, doubt and grief about your break-up into oblivion! The stronger and more centred you feel, the less room there is for these emotions and the negative thoughts that accompany them, and the less of a grip they can get on you as you try to move on.

30.

TAP INTO THE HEALING POWER OF CREATIVITY

In a magazine interview a few years back, Taylor Swift conceded that the only way she could pull herself out of the "awful pain of losing someone" was to write songs. Why? It helped her find clarity after a "crash-and-burn heartbreak". While I'm no songbird, I thoroughly believe unleashing your creativity can be one of the most powerful ways to overcome pain. It can do everything from channelling anger to soothing the mind. Not only can creative pursuits distract you from negative thoughts and make you feel a whole lot better (scientists have found that artistic engagement has significantly positive health effects), but many of us, me included, do some of our greatest, most inspired work in times of grief, frustration, anger and sadness.

So, open yourself up to your creative spark or streak, even if you feel like it's hard to find. Let it come to the surface – creeping or roaring – however it wants to appear. Pick up a pen, paintbrush, stick of charcoal, ball of clay, instrument, camera or whatever your medium of choice is and…

Let. It. Flow. Who knows what magic will come from your tortured soul?!

there is
only
ONE WAY
i will go:
FORWARD.

– LISA MESSENGER

UNSURE WHERE TO START? TRY THESE:

UNLEASH YOUR INNER CHILD

It's a crying shame that adulthood quashes our childish whims and imagination. Ask your inner little one what they'd like to do. Build a sandcastle? Climb a tree? Play marbles? (I still keep a bag of marbles in my office, just to remind me of the fun I had with them as a schoolgirl.)

MAKE SOME NOISE

Silence can be deafening and a recent study found being in a moderately noisy environment helps people be more creative. The optimal noise level matches the murmur and bustle of a coffee shop, so that's a good place to start if your art form is compact. If not, turn up the tunes.

CHANGE THE SCENERY

Nothing sparks inspiration like a new vista – book a weekend away in the country, the city or at the beach, or go the whole hog and head overseas on your own in search of new friends, places and a creative muse. If travel isn't an option, transport your office for the day to a library, park, graffiti-covered tunnel or tree-lined pavement.

LOG OFF

We're all guilty of reaching for our smartphones for company in moments of boredom, but as pretty as your Instagram feed might be, it is not only a time sucker, it also fills up all that beautiful empty space in your mind where creativity sits, latent. Kiss goodbye mindless scrolling to think, experience and explore. Try sketching, doodling or putting on some music instead.

MEDITATE ON IT

I discuss meditation in more detail in Step 29 so jump back if you missed it, because research shows that certain meditation techniques can promote creative thinking. So, embrace the opportunity to silence that busy mind. The meditation apps Headspace or The Mindfulness App are good places to start.

The idea for my very first book, *Happiness Is…*, came at a very painful time. In the midst of total dissolution and sadness, I went in search of exactly what made people happy, which resulted in a nation-wide pursuit and a best-selling book. If I didn't use my sense of defeat and failure to write that book, I would never have landed in publishing and then media, which has completely shaped my life today.

31.

CHOOSE YOUR ATTITUDE

you are responsible for how you face the experiences of life.

Life acts. You react. And, you can either choose a negative or positive reaction. While you can't change what has happened, your attitude is under your control and can always be changed.

32.

GET ACTIVE

There's nothing like some action to shake up those forlorn, scattered pieces of your broken heart and return the spark to your eyes and sweat to your brow. Feel like you just can't get pumped up about anything since your break-up? Worried that now the plans you two created together have been blasted into smithereens, there's literally nothing in your future to get excited about? It's time to lace up your trainers.

We know being active is a sure-fire way to boost your mood. Study after study backs this up, including recent research at Penn State that showed exercise increases feelings of excitement and enthusiasm – both qualities that are likely to be in short supply right now.

Getting into a regular exercise routine will also have the added benefit of increasing your confidence in your physical appearance – something which often takes a beating after a relationship ends.

33.

DON'T BE A
RELATIONSHIP BORE

Your family and friends love you, but…! Rehashing your relationship story over and over to them can keep dragging you back into the drama when your mind and body are ready to move on. And while they will happily listen, chat and offer advice, after the 99th re-run it will start to bore them to tears. The super lovely ones will continue to smile, cook you dinner and gently nudge you away from the topic. The more straightforward ones will call it. Either way, take their cues and use them for good – to shift your thinking and propel your focus.

Also, to be perfectly honest, as Emma Thompson says in *Love Actually*, "No one's ever going to shag you if you cry all the time."

And don't forget that *Sex and the City* episode in Season 2 when Carrie was obsessed with talking about Big, to which her friends finally snapped, saying, "Frankly, we can't take it anymore," and, "Look, we're as fu*ked up as you are. It's like the blind leading the blind."

34.
CREATE NEW MEMORIES

you
CAN'T
start the
next
chapter
of your life
if you keep
re-reading
your last one.

35.

START A NEW HOBBY

When an incredible friend of mine heard of my reak-up, they called with some wise words. One piece of advice was simply to start a hobby, but it was their motivation for doing so that inspired me. "Master at least one new thing so that your life is measurably richer than it was before the break-up," they suggested.

Hold up – step back and let that wisdom soak in.

If that resonates with you, if you've lost sight of personal goals or put things on ice because your partner wasn't as passionate about them as you were, NOW is the time to pick those dreams back up and create a better you. And when your mind is focused on standing up on a surfboard, it won't be wondering if you should have booked the trip to Greece you both talked about last year.

Go to a dance class
Audition for an amateur play
Learn a language
Learn to paddleboard or surf
Smash a couch to 5km running plan
Learn to code
Go to life-drawing classes
Join a tennis/netball/running club!
Do a typography course
Join a book club
Volunteer for a charity
Colour in (everybody's doing it!)
Start yoga classes
Collect something
Start a blog
Research insects
Become a mountain climber
Learn the ukulele

36.
ACHIEVE SOMETHING

This whole mess can wreak havoc with our daily routines – the by-products of sadness are usually reduced motivation and energy. As a result, you can find yourself hardly doing anything, let alone doing anything well.

It's likely you've recoiled from anything that's not life-and-death, opting for couch time over your spin class and takeaway over your grocery shop (hey, at least you're eating, right?). Then there's that growing tower of dishes, pile of laundry, the unreturned phone calls and trail of unopened emails clogging your inbox. While I'm all for going easy on yourself, especially in those early weeks, the problem with prolonging this behaviour is that it's cyclical. Lowering your activity level can lessen your motivation and make you even more lethargic. And when you stop doing the things you love and value, you also lose that buzz – the feeling of pleasure and reward – that your body and mind crave.

All of a sudden, things shift from a palatable pile of stuff you'll do later to a fiery ball of to-do stress that is gaining epic proportions and is rolling your way. Cry, stress, freak-out, cover up, ignore, avoid. What's the best way out of this lethal loop? Here's a small, yet powerfully practical tip: try completing something today – anything – so you can curl up in bed with a sense of achievement tonight, even if it's a small one. It will also be an injection of awesome into your self-esteem, which takes a battering during a break-up and can leave you feeling hopeless at just about everything. And… it helps you get back on track to creating a big, beautiful life for yourself with or without another human in the mix.

it always seems impossible until it's done.
– NELSON MANDELA

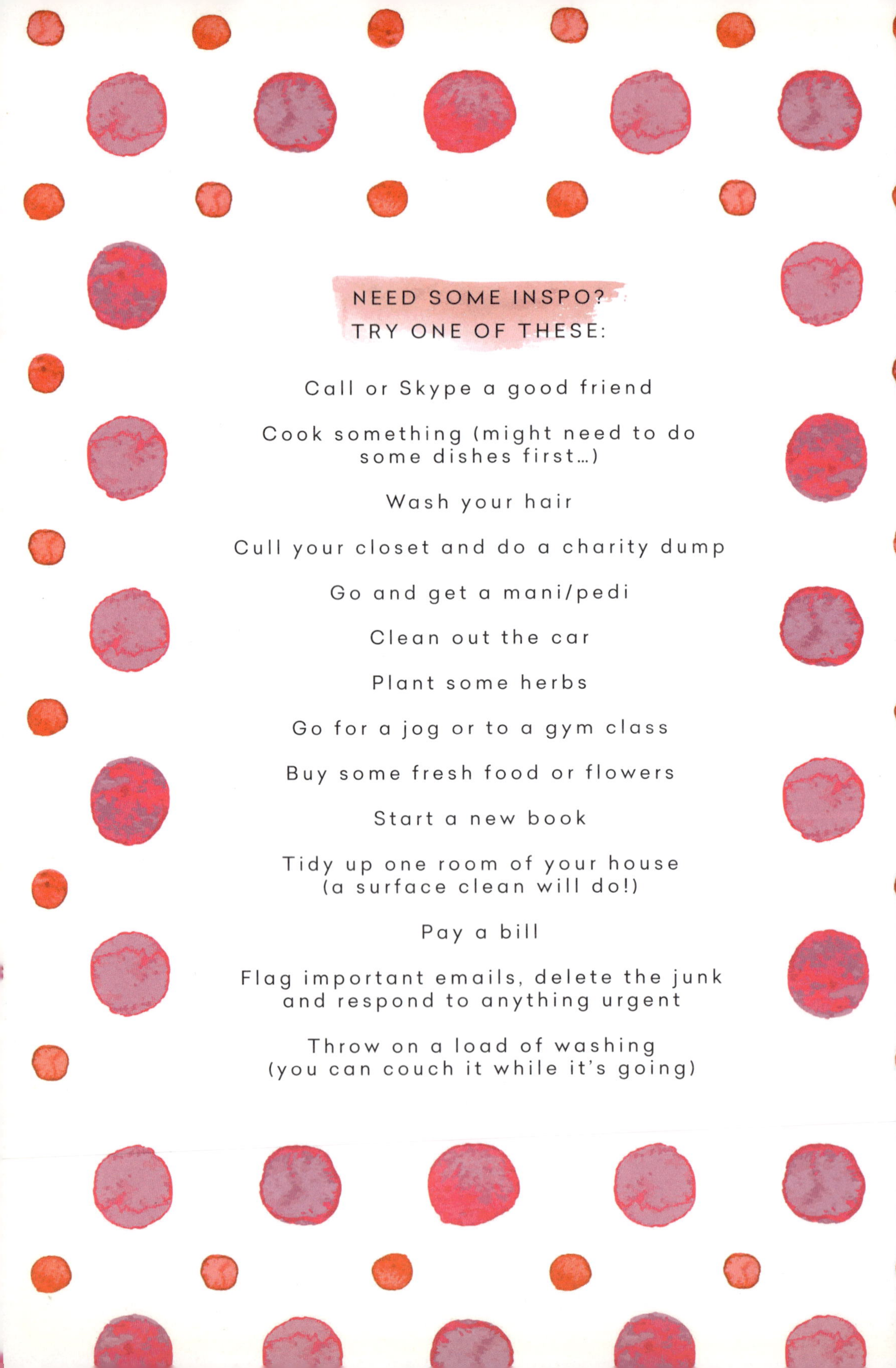

NEED SOME INSPO?
TRY ONE OF THESE:

Call or Skype a good friend

Cook something (might need to do
some dishes first…)

Wash your hair

Cull your closet and do a charity dump

Go and get a mani/pedi

Clean out the car

Plant some herbs

Go for a jog or to a gym class

Buy some fresh food or flowers

Start a new book

Tidy up one room of your house
(a surface clean will do!)

Pay a bill

Flag important emails, delete the junk
and respond to anything urgent

Throw on a load of washing
(you can couch it while it's going)

small steps
every day.

37.
CHOOSE JOY AND
PRACTISE GRATITUDE

Or… fu*k joy and fu*k gratitude!

There's a time and a place for everything, and yes, it's great – and important and ultimately gratitude should be the bedrock of everything – but there are some days when you just won't be feeling it. Instead, you'll feel like throwing your arms up in the air and saying, "Fu*k it all!" (Sorry about all the 'fu*ks'. One day during this break-up, a close friend said my use of the four-letter word was so exhaustive and creative that I should write a book on it.)

While I am a huge believer in gratitude for all things, I also believe there is such a thing as 'premature gratitude', when you shove a traumatic or intense emotional experience under the carpet with false gratitude, or you try and see it as a gift or lesson before you've really worked through the situation and the emotions it brought with it. It is okay to feel completely and utterly destroyed and grief-stricken for a time (see Step 9 about stages of grief and Step 6, which gives you a free pass to wallow in it for a little bit).

I think you need to fully feel what is going on first, so you can then experience, or at least move towards, authentic gratitude, and the truly deep sense of peace that comes with that. Otherwise, it can be empty and it certainly won't last. I have a little private ritual that unfolds in my life every day and I shared it with the world for the very first time in my book *Life & Love* but it's just as applicable now. All day, every day, hundreds of times, I say a little prayer of thanks as I go about my business. Just two little words: 'thank you'. Sometimes I whisper them, sometimes I just imagine them. I remember an important meeting I'd failed to schedule into my diary: thank you. I wake up in time to catch the sunrise: thank you. I find a car park easily on a busy day: thank you. It takes less than a second and I do it so often it's become subconscious, an innate, ingrained ritual I do without noticing. In the days and weeks immediately after this break-up, I didn't

stop this – I still found it easy to be thankful for the small blessings around me. BUT, it took me quite a bit of time to be thankful for the deeper issues at play. I got there, but I didn't rush myself. I didn't want the gratitude to be fake, what purpose would that serve? I would have been deceiving myself. You'll know when it's time to drag yourself up out of the grief pit to start looking once again at all the amazing blessings in your life. Think you're ready? Here are six ways to start feeling grateful again:

1. KNOW THE BENEFITS OF GRATITUDE.

"It is not happy people who are thankful, it is thankful people who are happy."
– Anonymous
Study after study shows how practising gratitude relieves sadness and stress. Dr Sonja Lyubomirsky, author of *The How of Happiness*, suggests we regularly set aside time to recall moments of gratitude (perhaps jotting them down in a journal or writing "gratitude letters"), to bolster our self-esteem and reduce stress.

2. BE MINDFUL OF NEGATIVE THOUGHTS AND ACT AGAINST THEM.

"Choose your attitude today. It's one thing you have complete control over."
– Anonymous
Just because you're feeling crap on the inside doesn't mean your actions have to reflect it. Here's the thing – you can actually encourage yourself to feel gratitude by 'acting' grateful. So force that smile at a stranger, or pick up the phone and thank your dad for his support.

3. SEEK OUT THE POSITIVES.

"Keep your face to the sunshine and you cannot see a shadow." – *Helen Keller*
It's all-too-easy to focus on the negatives when you're feeling low, but look up. Notice all of the little, positive things around you. The sun streaming through

your window (even just the fact that you have a window, if it's cloudy), that warm cup of tea, the neighbour who wheeled in your bin, your favourite song coming on the radio. Start small and you'll see there's so much to be grateful for.

4. LOOK ON THE FLIP SIDE.

"Always look on the bright side of life." – Monty Python

Finding those negative thoughts hard to quash? Write them down. Write down everything you don't like about your life and try to look at the list objectively. How can you flip these negatives around and turn them into positive outcomes? There's always a silver lining. Feeling miserable? Channel it into a creative project. Feeling lonely? Use this time to really focus on you, and your 'why'.

5. CONSIDER WHAT YOU HAVE TO LOSE.

"I cried because I have no shoes… until I saw a man with no feet. Life is full of blessings. Sometimes we're just blind to them." – Anonymous

Struggling to think of things to be grateful for? Look in the fridge. What would it be like if you didn't have any food? Or how would you feel if you didn't have your family around you, or your friends, or if that house of yours was taken away? Your car? Cat? What about your health? You might not be feeling so hot right now, but imagine living without your eyesight, or the use of your legs? Get some perspective by 'taking away' things you take for granted.

6. STAY IN THE NOW.

"Realise deeply that the present moment is all you ever have." – Eckhart Tolle

Chances are it will be hard for you to find gratitude in your past right now (your ex is there, after all), and the future you're imagining might be a little blurry (or scary!). So, keep your head in the present moment. Right here, right now. It's the only reality, after all, and if you are grateful for this very moment, you'll always live with gratitude.

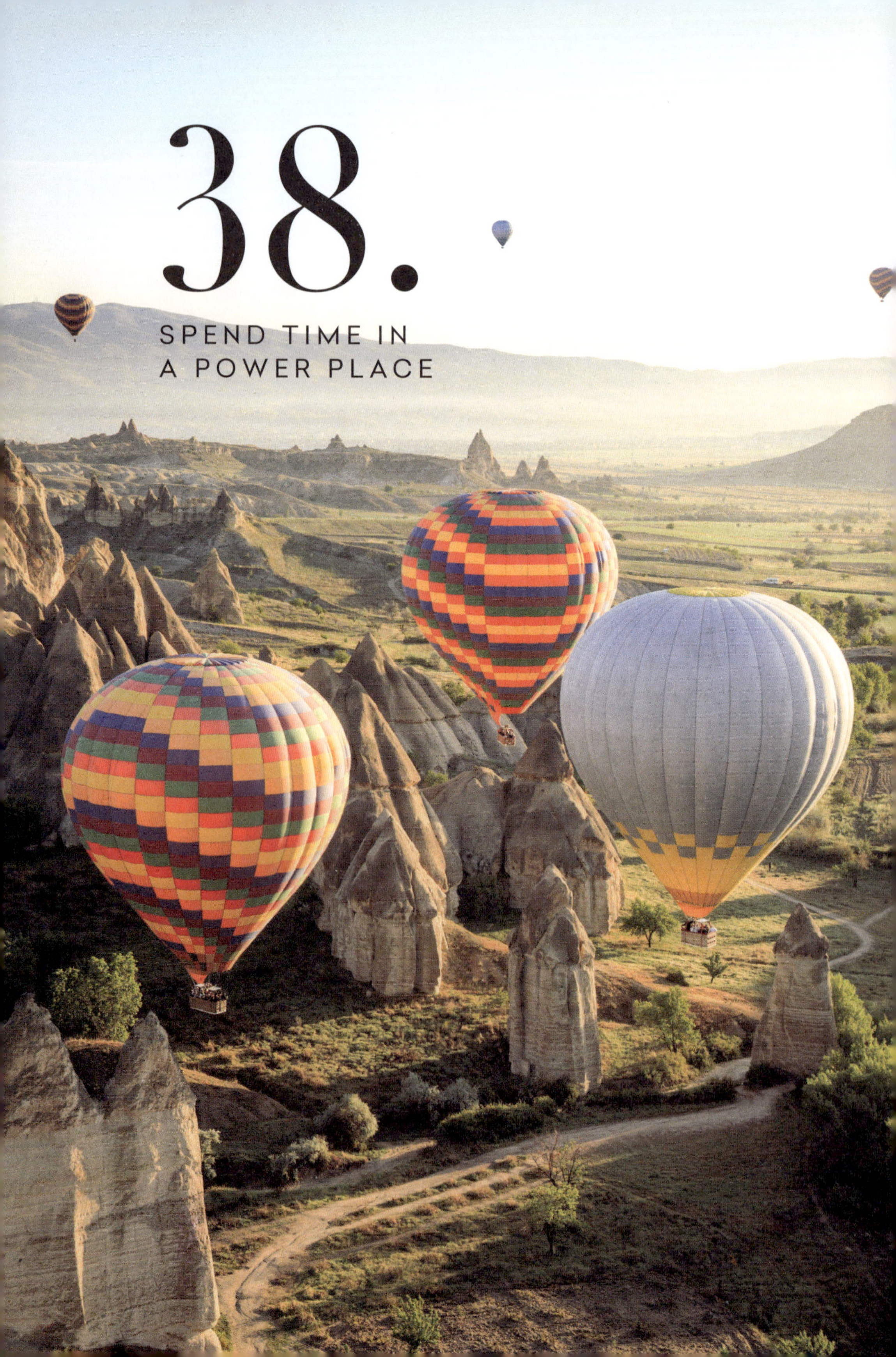

38.
SPEND TIME IN
A POWER PLACE

If you have a 'power place', make regular dates with yourself to go there.
If you don't have a power place, find one.

What do I mean? There is incredible power in having a place where you can go
to 'plug in' and walk away feeling energetically full, stronger and more empowered
to take on whatever life has thrown your way. It can bring you back to your
centre, help you reconnect with your purpose, your values, your inner strength
and your physical self, with incredible transformative capabilities.

IT MIGHT BE:

At the beach, with the fresh salt air on your face or waves washing over your body.
At the top of a mountain or nature look-out for perspective and solace.
In your car with the music pumping to jolt the senses and empower the mind.
At a church or temple for serenity and calm.
At home in your lounge room in the midst of a meditation.

Whatever the place, it will be unique to you. It will allow you to delve deep into
the parts of your being to shift any negative or challenging energy, so you
re-emerge ready to take the next step with greater confidence and momentum.
Go on, plug yourself in.

39.

CONQUER FEAR

When the Fear with a capital F kicks in – Fear of being alone; Fear of never finding love again; Fear of how the hell you're going to look after yourself, your kids/pets/plants etc. without him or her; Fear of surviving the (often toxic) social pressure – you know what to do: drink. Or have casual sex. Or run away to a cabin in the woods.

JUST KIDDING! Do not self-medicate (well, maybe occasionally is okay if you must, but try and do it with friends, and only when you're going to dance it off and have a really good friend to watch out for you. Not at home alone crying into the dog's fur…). And casual sex, well… we all know where that goes. A cabin in the woods is the better of the three options, but at some point you have to come back to reality.

Seriously, fear is paralysing and getting over it can be immensely challenging. Firstly, fear must be felt. Secondly, fear must be conquered if you are to move forwards.

In another of my books, *Daring & Disruptive: Unleashing the Entrepreneur,* I wrote an entire chapter on fear, and you can apply those principles to business or life generally. Here, I'll include a few small points. The brain is a truly powerful thing and if we let it, we can 'think' and 'project' fear until it paralyses us. But if that's the case, then surely we can 'think' and 'project' the opposite.

the only thing
we have
to fear
is fear
itself.
- FRANKLIN D ROOSEVELT

I have always loved this quote from the famous psychiatrist Karl Augustus Menninger, who says: "Fears are educated into us, and can, if we wish, be educated out." Another I refer to often is from the amazing Brené Brown, who once told Oprah, "We're all afraid. We just have to get to the point where we understand that it doesn't mean we can't also be brave."

More often than not, fear is perceived rather than real. Take the fear of being alone. You might be feeling anxious about the future, but what do you know to be true? Can you see into the future? Do you know that there'll never be another person for you? No. You can't possibly. There's no truth behind this fear whatsoever, so use the power of your mind and don't allow yourself to be wrapped up in this fear. Treat all fears you might have with equal scrutiny.

The first step is to get to the bottom of exactly what you're afraid of. Fear is also often ego-related, so be honest with yourself. Then you have something to work with.

Race straight to the worst-case scenario and stare your fear right in the face, thinking about how bad the situation could possibly be. Then, race back from there to the present moment, re-engineering the scenarios and evaluating the steps you could take at each juncture to avoid getting to the worst-case scenario. It's almost like a movie clip on high-speed reverse motion; a personal reconnaissance mission so you can spot the dangers and hypothesise. Then you are done. It can be that simple if you harness the power of your mind. And I believe you can.

renewal

40.

RETRIEVE YOUR SOUL

It can be so slow and steady that you didn't even realise it was happening, but more often than not, we lose sight of some parts of ourselves as a relationship unravels. There is a big difference between compromise, which every relationship needs a certain amount of to be sustainable, and sacrifice to the point of hugely important aspects of yourself getting lost, and with them, a vital part of your being. Usually these parts were what attracted you to each other in the first place, but it's amazing how much we change ourselves, and expect others to change themselves, without even realising until it's too late.

Don't underestimate the power of your life and being. If you feel you have drifted away from yourself during this relationship, embark on some soul retrieval.

Get your journal out and do this simple question-and-answer exercise:

1. Did I actually like who I had become in this relationship?
2. What part or parts of myself did I lose sight of during this relationship?
3. What do I need to regain and how can I do that?

You'll need to give yourself some time and space. This process can only be done by sitting with yourself.

you can be *soft* and *successful,* a traditionalist and a *rebel,* a lover and a *fighter,* vulnerable and *invincible.*

— LISA MESSENGER

be
yourself.
by yourself.
- LISA MESSENGER

Being alone doesn't mean sitting in an empty room. It can mean watching a great movie and having a bloody good laugh – or a bloody raw cry. It can mean facing your dark side or shadow self and coming out the other side raw and ragged but real and reborn.

This is something no friend can help you with – only you can get through the maze yourself and come out the other side changed. Slightly battered maybe, but stronger. And open. To whatever life brings you next. So, you need to get your power back and remember how amazing you are!

41.

STAY OPEN TO
FINDING LOVE AGAIN

"I'm never going there again!" we exclaim, and it's no wonder. "If this relationship isn't THE ONE, then I'm done!" (Cue the door to your heart slamming shut and the key being thrown away.)

Break-ups are hard. SO hard. They are full of painful, often toxic emotions that can run through our vital organs like a disease, destroying everything in their wake, and more devastatingly, our hope.

BUT… you have to resist the temptation of wallowing in this to the point where your heart is covered with a thick, rough, impermeable exterior that will stop you from being vulnerable to finding love again. It's a risk to open ourselves up to love, but the very notion of believing something wonderful could happen to you has the power to keep life exciting, even when it feels unbearable.

UNSURE HOW? TRY THESE:

1. STOP THE FLOW OF NEGATIVE THOUGHTS.

Thoughts like, "I will never love again" or "I will never be loved", but also the more sneaky ones like, "All my friends are getting married, except me" or "I am the only one at home on a Friday night". Remember, we are what we think.

2. FIGHT THE RESISTANCE AND CYNICISM WHEN OTHERS SPEAK OF LOVE OR EXPERIENCE IT.

Find tools that work for you personally. One of my staff told me she shoots her thoughts with a gun – I responded by saying I send mine away in a pink bubble, which sent us into roars of laughter, but both work for us. Cynicism can get ugly and it can also overtake your world before you even realise it is there.

3. BE A LOVER GENERALLY. Be warm to others, generous with your time and vulnerable in conversations – because we attract what we project.

4. REJECT COMFORT. Being vulnerable and open to others is hard and risky – even fraught with danger – so you must intentionally resist the temptation to stay within your comfort zone when it comes to love and relationships. Accept that date invitation instead of fleeing in fear, or continue the conversation that's getting a bit personal with a stranger or new friend instead of shutting it down.

5. ENJOY TODAY (AND EVERY DAY). Your time will come. For now, while romance eludes you, use this time to tick off a few personal goals, to catch up on things that may have slipped in your previous relationship or to become a better version of yourself generally.

As the saying goes… stay open to love and it will find you.

fall in
love
with your
future
because
it's yours to
create.

— LISA MESSENGER

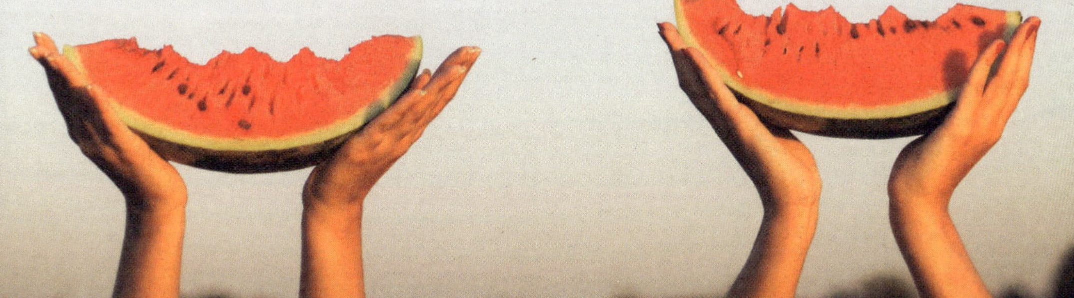

42.

SHIFT YOUR FOCUS

"Student says: 'I am very discouraged. What should I do?'
Teacher says: 'Encourage others.'" – *Anonymous*

Your best way forward is to stop thinking about yourself and look to others and the world around you. In the midst of a break-up, we can forget there are people far worse off than we are – enduring all sorts of injustices and atrocities. Sometimes switching on the news to gain some perspective is not a bad idea…

Yes, nurture yourself, yes, be kind to yourself and gentle on yourself, but remember that whatever you have going on, there is always someone else who could really benefit from your kindness and your love.

Extending this loving energy to someone else can only HELP you, and it will sure as heck help them! I have a friend who sometimes buys a lottery ticket. But she says every time she buys one, she involuntarily thinks, "Someone needs to win this more than me." It annoys the hell out of her that she thinks this, but even so, she realises that as she thinks it, she is acknowledging all of the blessings and abundance in her life and that her mind is fixed on others.

It's wonderfully empowering and can bring so much joy and lightness to put your focus onto other people, even in the midst of personal hardship. Many health experts say it's therapeutic and crucial to healing. After all, the wonderful charity Aussie Helpers, which supports farmers doing it tough on the land and has intervened in many suicide attempts, was started by a depressed farmer who decided to travel the country talking to those in a worse state than he was.

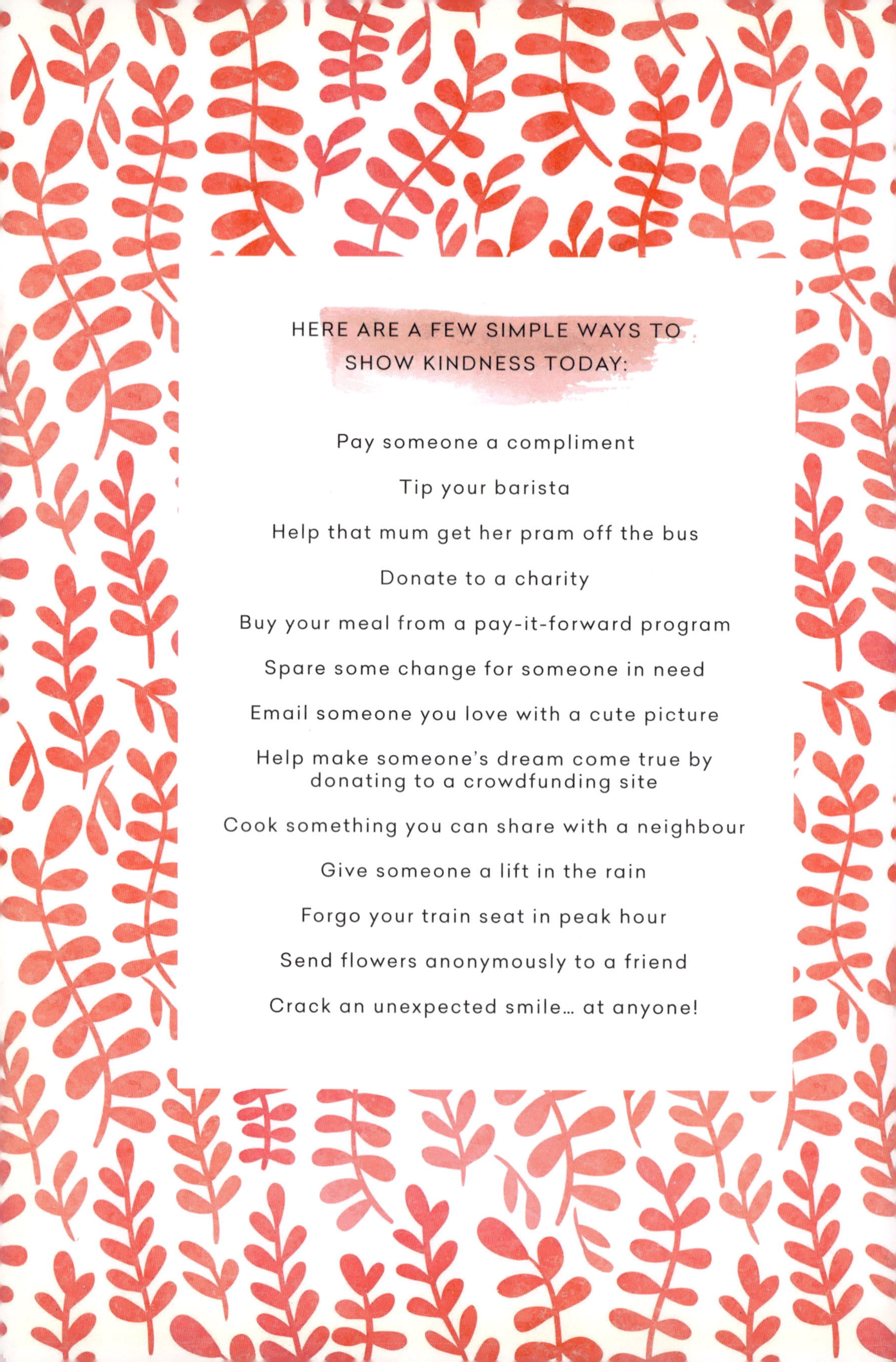

HERE ARE A FEW SIMPLE WAYS TO
SHOW KINDNESS TODAY:

Pay someone a compliment

Tip your barista

Help that mum get her pram off the bus

Donate to a charity

Buy your meal from a pay-it-forward program

Spare some change for someone in need

Email someone you love with a cute picture

Help make someone's dream come true by
donating to a crowdfunding site

Cook something you can share with a neighbour

Give someone a lift in the rain

Forgo your train seat in peak hour

Send flowers anonymously to a friend

Crack an unexpected smile… at anyone!

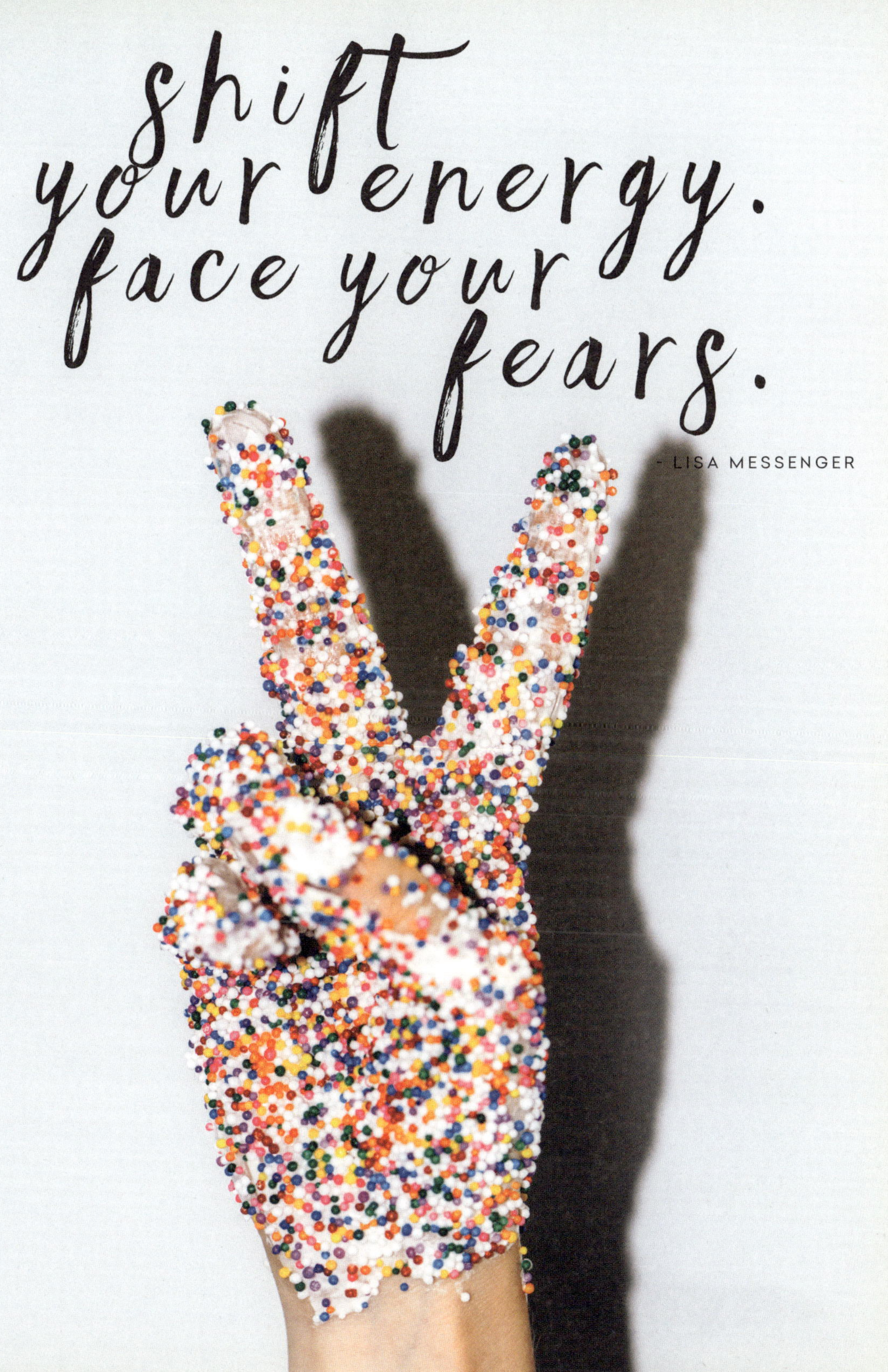

shift your energy.
face your fears.
- LISA MESSENGER

43.

DON'T REBOUND

Hmmmm… the rebound. Ouch. It's almost as bad as the 're-ride', which is when you go there again with your ex. The question is, is it really going to make you feel better?

I'm pretty sure for most people the answer to this question is a resounding "no", although I do acknowledge those (who can truly 'keep it casual') for whom the rebound can just be a sort of tension release. But the numbers show we're quick to bounce back, even if for the wrong reasons or without any real, long-term happiness. One survey carried out at the University of Missouri found 58 per cent of the brokenhearted questioned had slept with someone new within the first month of their break-up.

The end of a relationship is hard, and it's lonely, and with apps like OkCupid, Grindr or the all-too-easy Tinder at our fingertips, a 'quick fix' can be a mere right swipe away. But it's a dangerous game for you – mostly because you don't give yourself enough time to properly heal, meaning you won't fully deal with the grief or rebuild yourself on a healthy foundation.

Furthermore, it's hardly fair to the reboundee. Chances are you're not emotionally ready to handle another relationship yet and can end up hurting them, or you might struggle to really give of yourself and/or to trust in them fully, meaning the relationship will plateau. A rebound also invites unwelcome confusion (didn't you have enough going on in your head without adding another player to the mix?). And if you're trying to feel better about yourself, this approach won't work deep down inside your soul! You can't rely on others to boost your self-esteem – that's all up to you – you actually need this time to learn how to be happy again on your own. That can be tough to swallow, but you will thank yourself for taking the time to think, plan and renew.

So, hush all of those well-meaning friends who instantly try to get you 'back on the wagon' by setting you up with a friend or acquaintance, or encouraging that drunken hook-up, which seems like a really great idea on the back of five vodkas but the next morning feels… less than great (to put it politely).

Only you know how you feel, but experts warn against the rebound and the research backs it up. If you need time, take time. Don't rush into something to try and fill a gap that actually needs to remain unfilled for a time. Wait. And you'll be glad you did. When Mr or Miss Worth It arrives, you'll know.

H.O.P.E.

hold on,
pain
ends.

— ANONYMOUS

44.

SAY 'YES'

"Always say 'yes' to the present moment. What could be more futile, more insane, than to create inner resistance to something that already is? What could be more insane than to oppose life itself, which is now and always now? Surrender to what is. Say 'yes' to life – and see how life suddenly starts working for you rather than against you."
– Eckhart Tolle

What a beautiful, daring way to see the world and your place in it. If you've become cynical or resistant, try resetting your foundation by saying 'yes' to everything for a day, a week, or even a month. You might want to set a few boundaries for yourself: nothing illegal, harmful or against your values, but otherwise, liberate yourself. Go for that coffee, agree to the skiing trip or try the smoked eel when it's offered.

YEAH
YES
YES
Yes
YES SIM
Yes
SÍ
JA
Yup
Uh-Huh
Yeah
Yes

This is not about busying yourself – do not get busy for 'busy's sake' or you are just filling a void and not really dealing with and feeling the pain that will ultimately help you to move on. It's more about shifting your mindset away from negativity and the general state of grumpy blah that tag along with break-ups. By saying yes, you open yourself up to new adventures and new opportunities and let new people enter your life. Who knows what you miss out on by saying 'no?' (Think Gwyneth Paltrow in *Sliding Doors*.)

Rick Hanson, author of *Just One Thing: Developing a Buddha Brain One Simple Practice at a Time,* says we can learn from improvisational actors who have to go along with whatever scenario is handed to them on stage. "Real life is like improv: the script's always changing, and saying 'yes' keeps you in the flow, pulls for creativity, and makes it more fun," he says. "Try saying 'no' out loud or in your mind. How's that feel? Then say 'yes'. Which one feels better, opens your heart more, and draws you more into the world?"

It can often be terrifying to get yourself back 'out there' – especially when you're hurting like hell and you just want to curl up under the doona and make the world go away. But if you say 'yes' and turn up to something, even if just for five minutes, you're moving forwards. Or if you agree to do something wacky, it could make you laugh. And you need that right now. Say 'yes' – it's freeing. And you deserve that, now more than ever.

Go on… try it. "Yes, I will," you say. Now you're getting it.

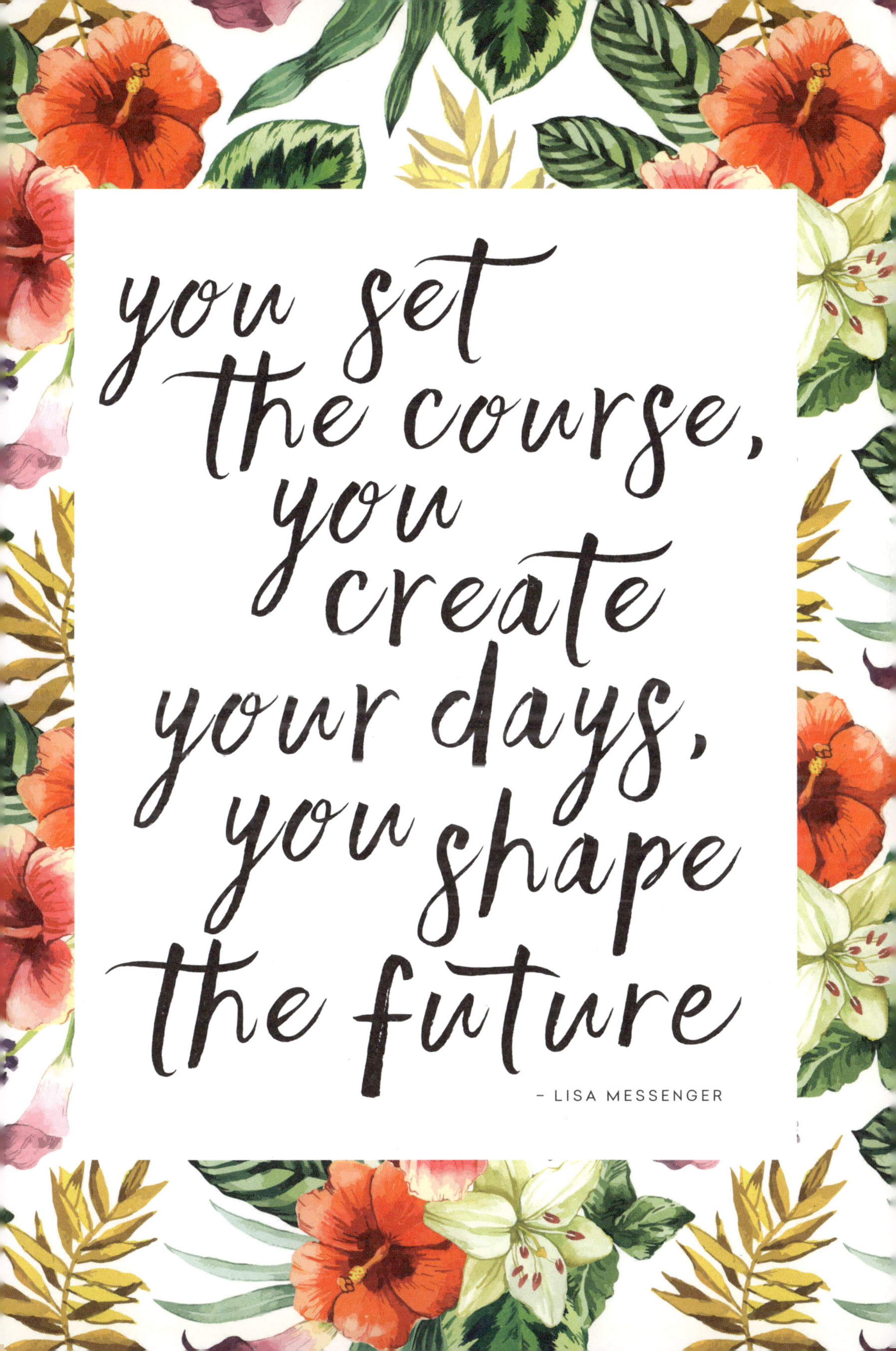

you set the course, you create your days, you shape the future
– LISA MESSENGER

45.
SEARCH FOR PURPOSE

PURPOSE.
your purpose.
your 'why'.
YOU.

When a relationship is all washed up and you've done all the crying you can do, there is no better time to switch the focus away from your partner and the relationship and back squarely on to you and your place in this big, wide, beautiful world.

In the midst of relationships, it's so easy to drift away from our true selves and lose sight of our 'why'. We can shift and bend to make a relationship work (even subtly) and change our core self in the process. We can get tied up in the plans and new direction of a relationship to the detriment of personal goals; again this can be in small ways and to do so is not necessarily a wrong move. We can get comfy, throw ourselves into the moment (go you!) and forget about personal resolutions that might have been previously made. Or worse, the relationship may have been toxic (sending love and light to you if that was the case) and your dreams were fully sabotaged along the way.

Whatever the case for you and your journey (even if you haven't drifted a single degree from yourself in this past relationship), one of the positives of a break-up is that it gives you space to reassess exactly where you are, examine what you're doing and question if you are on the right life path.

Ask yourself: "What's my 'why'? Why am I on this earth and how do I intend to live out my precious days for myself and others?" Then be brave enough to answer the question; it might be harder than you think and could take some time for clarity to surface. BUT, it is worth the process because there's nothing more exhilarating than feeling 100 per cent on track. It fuels your passion, gets you jumping out of bed in the morning, keeps you smiling, stimulates your mind, keeps you awake at night (for good reason), and helps you fight when things get rough (because they will). You can hang on to your 'why' in those moments as a compass, knowing that whatever comes your way, you have a job to do that is worth fighting for. And if you want more assurance, studies link having a life purpose with living longer, better mental health, better sleep, overall happiness and even less chance of developing Alzheimer's disease.

HERE ARE MY TIPS FOR FINDING YOUR PURPOSE:

✕ Know yourself. Understand your weaknesses, strengths, beliefs and values. Make discovering your purpose, your purpose. Imagine the impossible. That is enough.

✕ Stay open to opportunities and then experiment, experiment, experiment. Don't be afraid of failing.

✕ Believe you are good enough and that no one, and I mean no one, is better than you. You are not your past and you can create any future you want.

✕ Write down a list of people you admire and why. Adopt these traits as a way for you to show up in the world.

✕ Find a format you like for personal growth. It might be to educate yourself, train yourself, talk to others, network, find a great mentor, or to learn to replicate and duplicate with consistency.

✕ Develop a thick skin, personal strength and match fitness. These are imperative, so you can be grateful for rejection and see it as an experience instead of a paralyser.

✕ Know that at any moment in time, you can change your attitude. No matter your past failures or triumphs, you can have a positive mindset any time you CHOOSE.

✕ Develop a spectacularly different approach to everything.

✕ Be a trailblazer, break the rules, disrupt, take a different road and do it fearlessly.

✕ Set aside time to reflect, check-in and recharge. Fatigue can make cowards of us all.

✕ Notice how you feel. If you are 'on purpose', you will feel excited, exhilarated, full of adrenaline, alive and the very best version of yourself.

✕ Always be yourself. Stay grounded and remember where you came from.

✕ Just start.

AND AS YOU SEARCH FOR PURPOSE OR REALIGN YOURSELF TO YOURS ONCE AGAIN, REMEMBER THESE KEY POINTS:

- You are in control of your life and your happiness.
- You only get what you dream for.
- Your purpose is rarely just about you – there's a big world out there to make a difference in.
- Bring your entire self to the table when looking for your greater purpose: your work life, home life and social life. Don't try and separate it all out, let your purpose run through everything like a pulse.
- There can be new or renewed purpose – sometimes you will start something completely new, other times you'll simply realign yourself.
- When things go wrong, you can always go back and start again; just ensure you have the compass (that a-ha moment) so you know where 'north' is.
- Ditch the self-sabotage – it's your job to stay true to yourself, so don't let anything, anyone or any circumstance block you from hitting your stride.
- When you are in love again, look for someone who believes in your 'why' and will help you fulfil it; who will help you be the grandest version of yourself.
- Never hide who you truly are. Be proud of your plans because your untapped amazingness is worth fighting for and sharing with the world.

46.
VALUE YOURSELF

UNSURE WHERE TO START?
TRY THESE THREE IDEAS:

1. CARE ABOUT YOURSELF AS MUCH AS YOU DO OTHERS. Simply reverse the old adage and "Do unto yourself as you would do unto others." We rarely treat ourselves with the same compassion and tolerance as we would a friend or family member, so when negative thoughts start to come into your mind, ask yourself, would you say that about someone you care about?

2. AFFIRM YOURSELF. Take a look at everything you've achieved in your life and give yourself due credit. Better still, write it down. Are you a loving parent? Killing it in your career? Dedicated volunteer? Creative genius? On paper, you look pretty awesome, don't you? We can't rely on others for constant affirmation and validation (and if you ask for it, it will probably come across as you fishing for compliments to feed your ego). Instead, acknowledge all of the good you have done, and do it regularly. It's good for the mind and soul.

3. DO WHAT YOU'VE GOTTA DO. Figure out what else makes you tick. You could be a whiz in the kitchen, a top-notch netballer or kick-ass poetry writer. Whatever it is, allocate time in your schedule every week to DO IT. One of my team was recently at an appointment when the doctor took a call. He apologised, explaining that it was about his upcoming fishing trip. "It's not work-related," he confessed, "but crucial to my mental health." Never feel selfish for investing time in your wellbeing (and sanity!). You will feel better and you will like yourself more. You may even start to love yourself.

47.

DREAM

there is nothing like dreams for engendering the future.

– VICTOR HUGO

When you are awake and when you are asleep
Let your mind wander to those far-off places
Where reality doesn't matter
Where your heart leads the way
Where you smile from your depths
With the beauty of excitement
Where you roam free above it all
And soar deep within your soul

One of the first casualties of a break-up is your ability to dream. It's not that you can't, it's often that you don't think you deserve to. Set yourself free.

48.

HOLD LOVE IN A SACRED SPACE

there are
all kinds
of LOVE in
this world,
but never
the same
love twice.

If you have experienced deep love, it is really important to remember it, acknowledge it and treasure it.

People are capable of saying – and doing – truly terrible things to each other when they are hurting (think Michael Douglas and Kathleen Turner in the classic movie *The War of the Roses*), but clichéd as it sounds, time does heal wounds. No matter how hateful, destructive or toxic a break-up is, it is important to remember that once upon a time, you actually had real love for each other, and you can choose to keep that in a sacred space despite the fallout.

I believe this truly does help the healing.

Love and hate are simply two sides of the same coin – a coin that can be flipped either way in an instant when there are strong feelings and strong emotions. I've had some incredible relationships – from the crazy, passionate, youthful and speedy to the deeper and more mature. But... ALL OF THEM HAPPENED. And that is a fact that will never change.

In each relationship, you can – and we have – both moved on, but the love was real, it was sacred, and it was life-changing in many ways. So I honour it. And I honour those I was in love with. The fact that we ultimately weren't right for each other won't ever make that wrong, or less than it was.

Whatever the other may feel, I will always be grateful for that, and hold it sacred.

TO-DO LIST:

forgive myself.
love myself.
move forwards.
smile again.

- LISA MESSENGER

49.

THERE WILL
BE ANOTHER

As the shock wears off and the break-up dust settles, there inevitably comes that time when for a few scary hours (or days, or weeks) it can feel like a destiny awaits of long, lonely nights and dinners for one. If the thought "I'll never meet anyone else" has popped up in your head, know that *everyone* thinks this at some stage after a break-up. Also know this kind of thinking is a) all lies, of course and b) only producing more pain. If you would like romantic love back in your life at some point, then you need to renew your faith in love when you're ready, and start looking towards the future with a glimmer of hope and expectation in your eyes.

So, what's the best way to convince that wayward mind of yours that better things are, in fact, en route? Visualisation. Research shows that just thinking something – more specifically, visualising it in your head – has incredibly powerful effects. For example, an exercise physiologist called Guang Yue from Cleveland Clinic Foundation in the US found a group who regularly visualised themselves working out their biceps actually increased their muscle strength by 13.5 per cent, just by imagining their muscles moving! Feeling a bit toowoo-woo for you? I encourage you to be open-minded and to give it a go. Brain studies show that the thoughts we have produce the same mental instructions to the body as our actions. Visualisation affects a lot of cognitive processes in the brain, which means we are, in effect, training our brains to prepare for the real thing. And if you're really feeling daring, start a vision board with magazine clippings, pictures and quotes to help you 'see' exactly where you want to go.

It was Oprah Winfrey, a big visualisation advocate, who said, "Create the highest, grandest vision possible for your life, because you become what you believe." And it was actor Will Smith who says he saw himself as an A-list Hollywood actor long before the world did, also quoting Confucius about it: "He who says he can and he who says he can't are both usually right."

Here's how to put visualisation techniques into practice to help you move on from your break-up:

Find a quiet spot and start imagining, and seeing, yourself happy with a new partner. The key here is to make your vision as detailed as possible. Conjure up the smiles on both your faces. Ask yourself: What are we doing? What does he/ she smell like? How does he/she make me feel? Listen to what your heart is calling for, then let yourself see it happening on your mental movie screen (it's kind of like a choose-your-own adventure for your love life). Regular practice will make it even more powerful, until gradually you'll begin to believe, in the depths of your heart, that a bigger, brighter love is on its way. As our scientist friends have shown us, there's a mighty big chance your vision will come true.

believe
something wonderful
is going to happen*

*because it will.

the

end
beginning

further reading

There are hundreds of books and blogs out there to help you continue your journey to breakthrough and it's impossible to list them all. However, here are some that were particularly helpful for me or were recommended by trusted friends. I hope you find the insight, tools and power you need to propel you into greatness.

THE POWER OF NOW by Eckhart Tolle

Few people are able to join the dots like spiritual teacher Eckhart Tolle. He always gives you thought-provoking content, practical tips and enough space to work things out for yourself.

THE ALCHEMIST by Paulo Coelho

This truly amazing book is about transformation (not break-ups specifically) but gripped the world when it was first released and is just as powerful and relevant today.

ADD MORE ING TO YOUR LIFE by Gabrielle Bernstein

A true beauty, this self-confessed spirit junkie, motivational speaker and life coach has a no-nonsense, helpful way of getting her message across. This book is all about ridding your life of negative thought patterns and adding more happiness. There are great insights in here as you begin to create a new you post break-up. Also try Gabby's later books *May Cause Miracles* (about subtle shifts for radical change) and *Miracles Now* (tools for flow and finding your purpose).

HOW TO SEE YOURSELF AS YOU REALLY ARE
by His Holiness the Dalai Lama
This book is for anyone struggling with a sense of self and especially those prone to self-sabotage. It draws on ancient techniques from Tibetan monasteries and is centred on the fundamental Buddhist belief that love and insight connect for enlightenment like two wings of a bird. A beautiful analogy, isn't it?

EAT PRAY LOVE by Elizabeth Gilbert
This true story is about a woman who left her marriage (and her husband's expectations for children) to find herself again over a three-month trip to Italy, India and Bali. It's raw, funny and beautifully told and even if you've read it before, it's still the perfect life-isn't-over-after-a-break-up tale. When you're ready to move on, try Elizabeth's later book *Committed: A Love Story*, about the man she met in Bali who would eventually become her second husband, even though she vowed she would never marry again.

TINY BEAUTIFUL THINGS: ADVICE ON LOVE AND LIFE
FROM DEAR SUGAR by Cheryl Strayed
Thousands turned to Cheryl for advice as the anonymous Internet columnist 'Sugar' before she revealed who she really was. You'll laugh and cry reading this, but you will also find plenty of gems and parallels to make you think and reflect. Cheryl also penned the memoir *Wild*, which Reese Witherspoon later immortalised on the big screen.

SIX-WORD MEMOIRS ON LOVE AND HEARTBREAK
by Smith Magazine
The full title is *Six-word Memoirs on Love and Heartbreak by Writers Famous and Obscure*. This book, from the editors of *New York Times* bestseller *Not Quite What I Was Planning*, is essentially a collection of six-word confessions and is brilliant therapy.

BRIDGET JONES' DIARY by Helen Fielding
It was made into a motion picture for good reason. If you haven't read the book, lose yourself in its pages for the escapism and hilarity alone. It's soup for the broken soul.

THE BREAKUP BIBLE by Melissa Kantor
This is not a self-help book, but a novel about a break-up. Disclaimer: you'll probably cry but there is power in escaping into other people's pain to fully understand, appreciate or even unpack your own.

THE BREAKUP BIBLE by Rachel Sussman
Not to be confused with the novel above, this *is* a self-help book by Rachel, a psychotherapist, who suggests there are three key stages to every break-up.

IT'S CALLED A BREAKUP BECAUSE IT'S BROKEN
by Greg Behrendt and Amiira Ruotola-Behrendt
Greg co-authored the best-selling *He's Just Not That Into You* but this time, he teamed up with his wife for another dose of tough love. I do like that he promises to help you emerge from a break-up as a "superfox".

A GRIEF OBSERVED by C.S. Lewis

This is not for the faint of heart. It is a collection of Lewis' reflections on the death of his wife and was first published under a pseudonym in 1961. But as one of the most quoted thought leaders to this day, it's worth the pain – and subsequent renewal, focus and gratitude this book can bring.

STAG'S LEAP by Sharon Olds

This book of poems won the 2013 Pulitzer Prize for Poetry and was written to the backdrop of Sharon's life after divorce. You'll find courage and empowerment.

FALLING APART IN ONE PIECE by Stacey Morrison

Sometimes it's just reassuring to know someone has been through this before. Left with a new house, job and baby after divorce, Stacey's story uncovers surprising lessons of love, forgiveness and dignity.

GETTING PAST YOUR BREAKUP by Susan J. Elliott

Initially an attorney, Susan became a break-up and relationship coach after divorcing the father of her three children and losing her second husband to brain cancer. Her book is the perfect remedy for those who crave order in the chaos of break-ups, including the rules for going "no contact".

HAVE THE RELATIONSHIP YOU WANT by Rori Raye

When you feel ready to try love again, this book is worth a read before you even begin. Aimed at women, it can help you attract and retain Mr Right with long-term happiness.

acknowledgements

Even though this period of life was one of the hardest I have had to date, it ended up including some of the most beautiful moments of joy and love ever imagined – and that is because of the support and friendship I received; the most extraordinary silver lining of so many precious times shared with some extraordinary humans. It is another reason I am grateful for this passage of time, because without it, I would not have experienced those beautiful moments. To those who were there with me, I will cherish you and your care forever. It provided me with an unimaginable grounding for a beautiful path forwards.

TO MY BEAUTIFUL, KIND, LOVING COLLECTIVE HUB TEAM: you are absolute family to me, in every single sense of the word. I could not be more grateful. Getting to spend every day with some of the most fun, compassionate, authentic and loving people is just pure heaven for me. You loved me through some of my darkest hours; you made me laugh every day; you cried when I did; you took my side when I needed it and you gave me perspective on other days. Your strength, love and belief in our vision – and in me – has kept me going. Knowing we have a combined purpose and a 'why' and are working together to achieve that is the greatest reason to get up every day. Thank you Claire, Mel, Jade, Edie, Alex, Jessie, Tara, Mel D, Bec, Hannah, Phoebe, Tia, Michele, Kate, Lila, Nina, Sam, Nat, Georgia, Aimee, Mariela and Amy.

TO MY SISTER KATE: we have chatted daily at times and you have provided gorgeous strength and grounding. You also contributed a number of words to this book and helped me shape and mould it in its first iteration.

TO MY EXEC TEAM OF CLAIRE, MEL AND JADE:
you are the best friends I could possibly imagine and every day I am grateful
to have you by my side creating everything that is Collective Hub. I love and
appreciate that there is pretty much nothing you don't know about me holistically
and yet, you still adore me and stick by my side every single day. (And I you.)

**TO THOSE WHO FED ME AND POPPED IN
SPONTANEOUSLY:** my home has become your home and yours mine.
It's how I have always longed to live and this speed bump has been the greatest
catalyst for making it finally happen. Special shout-outs to Jules and Josh, Luke
and Aims, Billy and Fiona, Robbie and Dan.

TO MY EXTENDED A-TEAM: you give more strength than you
will ever know. Thanks Geoff B, BTG, Andy L, Samantha W, Cathie and Stu.

TO MY BEAUTIFUL FAMILY: Mum, Dad, Dennis and Margot.
And to Red and Vic for your incredible support in the early days. I will never
forget your extreme love and kindness.

**AND FINALLY, TO OUR BEAUTIFUL COLLECTIVE
COMMUNITY:** your outpouring of love has been unlike anything I have
ever experienced. Thank you. I was so overwhelmed, humbled and truly supported
– thanks for the jokes, book suggestions, blog posts, song lyrics and all manner of
things that came my way, which really did inspire and nourish me at a tough time.
In that moment, I realised how much a book like this was needed – so this is a
little about me, and hopefully a lot about giving back to you because few people,
I have discovered, can escape a break-up in their lifetime. Thank you for loving
me, Collective Hub and our vision. This, we hope, has been a little blip on the
path of something extraordinary. Onwards we go. xx

about the author

Lisa Messenger is the vibrant, game-changing Founder and Editor-in-Chief of
The Collective as well as CEO of publishing house The Messenger Group. *The
Collective* is an entrepreneurial lifestyle magazine distributed into over
37 countries with a mandate to disrupt, challenge and inspire. In addition, she
has worked globally in events, sponsorship, marketing, PR and publishing.

Lisa has authored and co-authored 16 books and become an authority in the
start-up scene, charting her rollercoaster ride to success in best-selling book
Daring & Disruptive: Unleashing the Entrepreneur and its sequels *Life & Love:
Creating the Dream*, which reached #1 on Booktopia and *Money & Mindfullness:
Living in Abundance.* With fans including Sir Richard Branson and *New York
Times* best-selling author Bradley Trevor Greive, Lisa's vision is to build a
community of like-minded people who want to change the world.

Her passion is to challenge individuals and corporations to change the way
they think, take them out of their comfort zones and prove that there is more
than one way to do anything. She encourages entrepreneurial spirit, creativity
and innovation. She pinches herself as to how incredible her life is, but is also
acutely aware and honest about life's bumps and tumbles along the way.

Lisa has a fascination for continual growth and in between being a serial
entrepreneur and avid traveller, spends most of her time in Sydney with
her beautiful dog, Benny.

   @lisamessenger #lisamessenger

collective hub

Collective Hub launched in 2013 as a print magazine, but quickly became a global sensation that is now sold in 37 countries.

A few years on, we have evolved into a true multimedia brand that also encompasses engaging digital platforms, one-of-a-kind events, strategic collaborations and unique product extensions.

Across it all, our unwavering vision is to uplift and empower our community to live their fullest lives.

We combine style and substance with a fresh perspective on the issues that matter – across business, design, technology, social change, fashion, travel, food, film and art.

Whether you are looking for a creativity boost, professional advice from industry experts, the most exciting places to experience or a warm and practical pep talk, we believe Collective Hub can be your ultimate guide to making an impact in the world.

COLLECTIVEHUB.COM

@lisamessenger #lisamessenger
@collectivehub #collectivehub

other books by lisa

COLLECTIVEHUB.COM